DADDY'S DYIN'
(Who's Got The Will?)

A Comedy in Two Acts

By
DEL SHORES

SAMUEL FRENCH, INC.
45 WEST 25TH STREET   NEW YORK 10010
7623 SUNSET BOULEVARD HOLLYWOOD 90046
LONDON   TORONTO

IMPORTANT BILLING AND CREDIT REQUIREMENTS

All producers of DADDY'S DYIN' *must* give credit to the Author of the Play in all programs distributed in connection with performances of the Play and in all instances in which the title of the Play appears for purposes of advertising, publicizing or otherwise exploiting the Play and/or a production. The name of the Author *must* also appear on a separate line, in which no other name appears, immediately following the title, and *must* appear in size of type not less than fifty percent the size of the title type.

For Mama Merck

Rex Knowles and Del Shores
present

DADDY'S DYIN'
WHO'S GOT THE WILL?

Written by
Del Shores

Directed by
Sherry Landrum

Summer -- 1986
Lowake, Texas
The Turnover family living room

ACT ONE
Scene 1: mid-afternoon
Scene 2: two hours later
Scene 3: early next morning

ACT TWO
Scene 1: later that afternoon
Scene 2: one hour later
Scene 3: mid-morning; three days later

There will be a brief intermission between acts.

Cast in order of appearance

Sara Lee Turnover	Judith Durand
Lurlene Turnover Rogers	Glenda Tremaine
Mama Wheelis	Molly McClure
Evalita Turnover	Rosemary Alexander
Harmony Rhodes	Michael Hoit
Buford Turnover	William Edward Phipps
Orville Turnover	Mickey Jones
Marlene Turnover	Patrika Darbo

DADDY'S DYIN' (WHO'S GOT THE WILL?) was originally produced by Rex Knowles and Del Shores in association with Jeff Murray and Nicolette Chaffey for Theatre/Theater in Hollywood, California, February 7, 1987. It was directed by Sherry Landrum; the set was by Newell Alexander; and costumes were by Eleanor Hurt. The production stage manager was Cheryl Correll, assisted by Denise Lowe, John Dickey and Tara Tremaine. The associate producer was Kelley Alexander. The cast, in order of appearance, was as follows:

Sara Lee Turnover. . . . . Judith Durand
Lurlene Turnover Rogers . . . . Glenda Tremaine
Mama Wheelis. . . . . Molly McClure
Evalita Turnover. . . . . Rosemary Alexander
Harmony Rhodes. . . . . Michael Hoit
Buford Turnover . . . . William Edward Phipps
Orville Turnover . . . . Mickey Jones
Marlene Turnover. . . . . Patrika Darbo

Also appearing in various roles during the long run were: Newell Alexander, Peter Alexander, Samantha Harper, Brenda Hillhouse, Sarah Hunley, Suzanne Hunt, Ida Lee, Ernie Lively, Dan Livingston, Frances Marshall-Labyorteaux, Lonna Montrose, Coleman Moss, Betty Murphy, Sonny Shroyer, Del Shores, Catherane Skillen, LaRue Stanley, Don Starr, Dennis Tufano, Greg Webb, Cheryl Correll, John Dickey, Denise Lowe, Mary Garripoli and Noreen Reardon.

DADDY'S DYIN' (WHO'S GOT THE WILL?) was originally produced in an Equity production by Grant Walpole for Pioneer Square Theatre in Seattle, February 25, 1988. It was directed by Sherry Landrum, the set was by Peggy McDonald; costumes were by Marienne O'Brien; light design was by Dustin Wall; property design was by Ken Crump; and sound design was by Nacho Bravo. The production stage manager was Kenny Telesco and the technical director was Annalee Purdy. The cast, in order of appearance, was as follows:

Sara Lee Turnover	Barbara Benedetti
Lurlene Turnover Rogers	Gwen Overland
Mama Wheelis	Lyn Tyrrell
Evalita Turnover	Mike Murphy
Harmony Rhodes	Robert Nadir
Buford Turnover	Robert Munns
Orville Turnover	Jim Dean
Marlene Turnover	Laura Kenny

THE CAST

SARA LEE TURNOVER, 36, the middle sister. Twenty pounds overweight, the town beautician, sports a bleached beehive. Single and still lives at home. Strong-willed and has a wonderful sense of humor.

LURLENE TURNOVER ROGERS, 42, the oldest sister. A preacher's wife and elementary school teacher. Attractive, stylish, very Christian—but she has a bite.

MAMA WHEELIS, 80, the Turnover children's grandmother. She's fiesty, speaks her mind, and rules the household.

EVALITA TURNOVER, 35, the youngest sister. Six-times married, loves to shock her family. She was a beauty—and still is from a distance. Has a worn look about her. A wounded soul.

HARMONY RHODES, 36, Evalita's latest fiance. A musician and vegetarian. Attractive, tan, off-beat, long curly hair. Looks like Jesus with earrings. Has a past.

ORVILLE TURNOVER, 38, the brother. Fat, abusive, unhappy and mean. A redneck trash collector.

BUFORD "DADDY" TURNOVER, 67, the father. A stroke victim. Partially paralyzed on his left side, but can walk with a slight limp. Has occasional moments of coherency.

MARLENE TURNOVER, 36, Orville's wife. Temporarily overweight. A constant victim of Orville's abuse. However, losing sixty-two pounds can boost a girl's confidence.

AUTHOR'S NOTE: These people are real, not cartoons. It's easy to go for the laughs, it's harder to strive for the truth.

THE SETTING

The action of the play takes place in the living room/dining area of the Turnover farmhouse, one-half mile outside of Lowake (pronounced Lo-way-kee), Texas.

THE TIME

Summer, 1986.

DADDY'S DYIN'

ACT ONE
SCENE 1

*The PHONE is ringing as the LIGHTS come up on the living
room/dining area of the Turnover farm house. Downstage is
the living room. It is pretty basic, with a sofa, chair, piano,
lots of pictures and knick knacks, and a coat closet. Upstage
is the dining area with a table, chairs, and a picture of the
Lord's Supper over the table. There are entrances to the
kitchen, the hallway, and to the front porch. SARA LEE
TURNOVER, 36-years-old, about 20 pounds overweight, the almost pretty middle sister comes out of the
kitchen, checks her beehive hairdo in the mirror and then goes
for the phone.*

SARA LEE. Hold your taters. I'm comin', I'm comin'.
Hello. Oh, hello, Maybelline. Ma...Ma...May...Maybel-
line— now jest hold on a minute before yew go off on a
rampage, I can't talk right now. *(Pause.)* Ma...Ma...Maybel-
line— I don't give a flyin' flit about ol' Lady Barnes and
'er vericose veins operation. I'm tickled pink they
stripped the thangs, but I got my own problems. Daddy's
comin' home from the hospital today and ever'body's
comin' in ta watch 'im die. *(A car drives up and a DOOR
SLAMS.)* Oh shit— there's one of 'em now. *(Looks out the*

9

window.) It's Lurlene. I gotta quit sayin' shit. Listen, Maybelline, I'll call ya later. Bye, bye. *(MAYBELLINE keeps talking; desperate.)* Maybelline, I gotta go. *(She hangs up, and frantically checks the room, runs and opens the Bible on the coffee table, turns on the radio and switches the station from country to gospel, and there is a KNOCK at the door. She answers it; LURLENE, the 42-year-old, saintly, attractive, oldest sister walks in.)* Lurlene! *(They hug.)*

LURLENE. Oh, Sara Lee. It's so good to see you. *(looking around)* And it's so good to be home. Oh, that music is so soothing.

SARA LEE. *(a touch of sarcasam)* I know it gits me through life. I jest finished my daily devotional. *(Indicating Bible; she turns the radio off.)*

LURLENE. How is he, Sara Lee?

SARA LEE. Not too good, Lurlene. Come on in and sit down. Yew must be exhausted after that drive. *(They sit.)*

LURLENE. So what did Dr. Wetzel say?

SARA LEE. He sed that Daddy has what they call progressive stroke and the next one's pro'bly gonna kill 'im. There idn't enythang else they can do about it. It's real sad, Lurlene. He's crazier than a bed bug. *(She goes and turns up the window unit air conditioner.)* Lord have mercy, it's hot. This ol' air conditioner ain't doin' a lick a good.

LURLENE. I should of come sooner. Where's Mama Wheelis?

SARA LEE. She walked over to the Pig to git some groceries.

LURLENE. The Pig. I haven't heard that in years. We don't have Piggly Wiggly's in Roma.

SARA LEE. Oh, our's is real nice now. They re-modeled—added on to the back, yew know. They even carry yogurt. Yew want some coffee? *(She gets up and Exits in the kitchen.)*

LURLENE. *(Stands in front of the air conditioner.)* I'd love some. Cream, no sugar.

SARA LEE. I remember. *(from the kitchen)* How's the Reverend and the boys?

LURLENE. Fine. J.D.'s preaching a revival in Rio Grande City. I sure hated to leave right in the middle of it. We already had two rededications and one profession of faith.

SARA LEE. *(Returning with the coffee.)* Well, praise the Lord!

LURLENE. *(Returns to her seat.)* We do, Sara Lee. I hope you weren't being facetious.

SARA LEE. Well, I hope I wadn't either seein's it sounds like somethin' I wouldn't wanna be doin'.

LURLENE. I meant I hope you weren't making fun...

SARA LEE. Aw, no. I been goin' to church myself lately. Even hit the choir a coupla times. I sang alto.

LURLENE. Oh, I'm so glad you're back in church again. My prayers have been answered.

SARA LEE. Aw, shit, Lurlene—whoops. *(Covers her mouth.)* See there. I'm still in the early stages of gettin' back my religion.

LURLENE. Oh, I almost forgot. I brought you some pictures of my boys. *(She fumbles through her purse and takes out her wallet and gives some pictures to SARA LEE.)*

SARA LEE. *(looking at pictures)* God, I feel old. Last time I seen them kids they was barely outta diapers. I wish ya'll had come around more.

LURLENE. *(Trying to avoid the subject.)* When did you say the others are coming in?

SARA LEE. They're all on their way. *(Still looking at pictures.)* They sure are good lookin', Lurlene. Orville should be here about five. And Evalita sed she'd be here after lunch. I hope nothin's happened. *(She puts the pictures in the photo album on the coffee table.)*

LURLENE. Well, you know Evalita. She'll be late to her own funeral. It'll be nice...everybody together again.

SARA LEE. It'll be a livin' hell and yew know it.

LURLENE. I know. People do change, Sara Lee.

SARA LEE. Yeah, Evalita changes husbands and hair colors and Orville changes at least two sizes a year.

LURLENE. *(laughing)* Oh, stop it. *(still laughing)* That's not funny.

MAMA WHEELIS. *(Yelling O.S. as she is approaching the back door in the kitchen.)* Hey, git outta my garden. I mean it. Scat. Now stop it. Right now. Sam, stop it...

LURLENE. Mama Wheelis.

MAMA WHEELIS. *(O.S.)* I'm gonna git my double barrel shotgun and kill me a hound. Quit that...I mean it. Git outta my tamaters.

LURLENE. Shh. I'm going to surprise her. *(She hides in the coat closet, waiting for MAMA WHEELIS; SARA LEE Exits into the kitchen.)*

MAMA WHEELIS. Don't yew come over here waggin' that tail. Whoa...git offa me...stop it...yure paws are muddy. Stop it. Whoa. *(calling out)* Sara Lee, come hep me. Dad burn it. Stop lickin' me. That dun it. *(yelling)* Yew brang me back them sausage links.

SARA LEE. (O.S.) What's wrong, Mama Wheelis? Git

outta here, Sam. Go home.

MAMA WHEELIS. *(O.S.; overlapping)* Brang me the shotgun. I'm gonna kill me a mutt.

(Entering the kitchen doorway, she is their grandmother, 80ish, spry and feisty.)

MAMA WHEELIS. Dad burn it. I'm gonna call Clara Bell Ivey and give her a piece of my mind. Dad burn it. Tore my knee highs. That ol' heinz fifty seven mutt a hers, Sam, tore up my garden, uprooted my tamaters and took off with my sausage links. And I paid a dollar-thirty-seven fer these knee highs. Honey, put them groceries up, please. *(She walks into the living room talking a mile a minute.)* There oughta be a law. I'm gonna warn her one more time to keep that mutt tied up, then I'm gonna kill 'im.

(LURLENE jumps out of the closet.)

LURLENE. Mama Wheelis! *(MAMA WHEELIS lets out a big scream, scared out of her wits.)* It's me, Mama Wheelis, Lurlene.

MAMA WHEELIS. Yew scared the livin' daylights outta me. *(Hugs her.)* Oh, baby, I ain't seen yew in a coon's age.

LURLENE. It's been too long. *(Hugs her tight.)* Oh, I've missed you. ·

MAMA WHEELIS. *(almost emotional)* I've missed yew too, baby. What was yew doin' in that closet?

(SARA LEE sticks her head in the doorway.)

SARA LEE. Mama Wheelis, yew want this chicken in the deep freeze?

MAMA WHEELIS. Naw, honey, leave it in the 'frigerdare. I'm gonna make chicken and dumplin's fer dinner tamarrow. Did yew check my roast while I was gone?

SARA LEE. *(Entering the living room.)* Yes ma'am, I did.

MAMA WHEELIS. The thermameter down at the Pig sed 103...in the shade. I got the pertiest roast down at the Pig yesterdey. It's in the oven, been cookin' all day. And I made cobbler. Clement Barnes give me some fresh peaches from the tree in 'is back yard. Sara Lee, did yew do that dye job on Cookie Hawkins' hair? I seen 'er in the Pig and 'er hair is as pink as a Easter egg.

SARA LEE. New, she musta done it 'erself. I *am* a highly trained professional, thank yew very much. *(Pats her beehive.)*

MAMA WHEELIS. Last month it was blue. She oughta leave it alone. She cain't see good enough ta know it don't look good. God bless 'er.

LURLENE. She must be close to ninety. I'm surprised she's still around.

MAMA WHEELIS. Lord, honey, she's crippled over sa bad with artheritis she cain't hardly walk. Still has a sense a humor though. Told me the other day that she had a date two nights in a row. Jest as straightfaced as she could be. Sed Fridey night she went out with Arthur and Saturdey night she went out with Ben. I asked 'er, "Arthur and Ben who?" and she sed, "Arthur Itis and Ben Gay." I 'bout hit the floor. Ain't that a good 'un? Arthur Itis an

Ben Gay. *(LURLENE appreciates the joke; SARA LEE doesn't.)* That ol' Cookie's a card. Bless 'er heart.

SARA LEE. I heard that story about a million times already.

MAMA WHEELIS. Well, smartie mouth, cover yure ears if yew don't wanna listen. Lurlene ain't heard it. *(laughing)* Arthur Itis and Ben Gay.

LURLENE. How's Mrs. Finwick?

MAMA WHEELIS. Oh honey, she's dead. Was eat up with cancer.

LURLENE. Oh, I'm sorry.

MAMA WHEELIS. Bless 'er heart.

SARA LEE. I wonder what's keepin' Evalita. I'm a little worried.

MAMA WHEELIS. I wudn't worry none about her. She probably stopped at a roadside park to look fer a new husband. Jest got divorced agin. I've lost count.

SARA LEE. I thank this was number six.

LURLENE. Oh, my word.

SARA LEE. Now, Mama Wheelis...yew remember our little talk.

MAMA WHEELIS. Yes, I remember our little talk. But let me remind yew missy that I am the grandmother here and yew are the granddaughter. So don't yew tell me how ta act.

LURLENE. Evalita stopped answering my letters. I was surprised she agreed to come.

SARA LEE. I wadn't. And Mama Wheelis, I ain't tellin' yew how to act. I was just tryin' to give yew some suggestions on how ta git along with her.

MAMA WHEELIS. Well, since leavin' town seems to be

outta the question, I'll jest make do. Lurlene, Nigger Pajoe's real bad. 'Member Nigger Pajoe, used to shine shoes down at the barber shop?

SARA LEE. *(scolding)* Mama Wheelis! I have asked yew over and over not to use that word. It's offensive.

MAMA WHEELIS. I don't mean nothin' by it. That's what he calls himself. What am I supposed ta call 'im?

SARA LEE. I give up.

LURLENE. He was always such a sweet man.

MAMA WHEELIS. I take 'im a plate lunch ever' day. He don't have no fam'ly left.

LURLENE. Poor thing. *(pause)* The last time I saw Evalita it was summer and she and the girls came down to see us. She was in between husbands. I didn't think about it, but I had a picture of Evalita, Jack and the girls on my dresser and...

MAMA WHEELIS. *(interrupting)* Jack was the best husband Evalita ever had.

LURLENE. She was so mad. I don't think she ever forgave me. Then about a year ago she stopped answering my letters right after she married that foreign guy.

MAMA WHEELIS. Needed his citzenship papers. That's the only reason he married 'er. Evalita thought he had money. *(Checks the air conditioner.)* Lord, it's hot in here.

LURLENE. I just couldn't bring myself to go to that wedding.

SARA LEE. *(Picks up the photo album and finds a picture.)* I couldn't neither. But she sent pictures. *(Shows it to LURLENE.)* Married in white...agin.

MAMA WHEELIS. I don't know who she thinks she's foolin'. She's about as pure as mud.

SARA LEE. Number five and married in white. Daddy went and gave her away...agin.

LURLENE. Again?

MAMA WHEELIS. She cain't do no wrong in Buford's eyes.

LURLENE. Well, I guess we shouldn't judge. *(starts laughing)* But it is hard. *(getting up)* I could certainly use a fresh cup of coffee.

MAMA WHEELIS. Here, honey, I'll git that.

LURLENE. *(Anticipating MAMA WHEELIS' response.)* Is this Folgers?

MAMA WHEELIS. *(Trying her best to imitate.)* The richest kind, baby. Yew know me and Miz Olsen...vee go vay back. *(Takes her cup.)* I'll fix ya a fresh cup.

LURLENE. Thank you.

MAMA WHEELIS. *(As she Exits.)* Arthur Itis and Ben Gay.

LURLENE. She hasn't changed a bit.

SARA LEE. She's a character alright. 'Bout drives me crazy, but I don't know what I'd do without 'er.

MAMA WHEELIS. *(from kitchen)* Did yew tell 'er the big news, Sara Lee?

SARA LEE. Not yet.

LURLENE. What news?

MAMA WHEELIS. Tell 'er, Sara Lee.

SARA LEE. Okay. Lurlene, Clarence and me's fin'ly gittin' married.

LURLENE. You're what?

SARA LEE. I ain't gonna be a old maid after all, Lurlene.

LURLENE. Oh, Sara Lee, that's wonderful. *(They hug.)*

I'm so happy for you.

SARA LEE. I thank he's changed, Lurlene. Clarence tried to git me ta git a real big diamond, but I jest couldn't see spendin that kinda money on a ring. We picked it out together. *(pause)* I wanted Daddy ta give me away.

LURLENE. It's real pretty.

(A car pulls up outside. MAMA WHEELIS re-enters with coffee.)

SARA LEE. Oh, my Lord. There's someone now. *(She runs and looks out the window.)*

MAMA WHEELIS. Is that Buford and Orville?

SARA LEE. Naw, Mama Wheelis. It's Evalita.

MAMA WHEELIS. Well, spit in the fire and call the dawgs!

SARA LEE. Good Lord, she's in a panel truck with a sign painted on it. It sez, "The Evalita Turnover Band." And she's got a hippy with 'er. *(MAMA WHEELIS and LURLENE rush to look out the window.)*

LURLENE. I'm a little nervous. I haven't seen Evalita in five years.

MAMA WHEELIS. "Count yure many blessin's name them one by one."

SARA LEE. Now, Mama Wheelis, behave yureself.

MAMA WHEELIS. Don't tell me how ta behave. I'll behave like I want. There are some advantages to being old besides Social Security.

(There is a knock on the door. SARA LEE answers the door. EVALITA, the youngest sister, 35-years-old, very attractive in a worn-out way, dark purple hair, dressed in cut-off jeans and a

halter, walks in with HARMONY, her fiance, mid to late 30's, long hair, wearing a few earrings, torn jeans and an open, sleeveless, jeans jacket, with no shirt under it and barefooted.)

SARA LEE. Evalita! *(They hug.)*

EVALITA. Sara Lee!

SARA LEE. Looky here, ever'body. It's Evalita...

EVALITA. And Harmony. This is my fiance, Harmony Rhodes...

MAMA WHEELIS. *(Giving HARMONY the once over.)* Lord have mercy.

EVALITA. *(Spotting LURLENE.)* Lurlene! *(They hug.)*

LURLENE. Hello, Evalita. You look...real good. *(She shakes HARMONY'S hand.)* Harmony, I'm Lurlene... Evalita's oldest sister.

HARMONY. Oh yeah, the Bible thumper.

LURLENE. The what?

EVALITA. *(Pokes HARMONY.)* Harmony! He was jest kiddin', Lurlene.

HARMONY. *(Hugs EVALITA tight.)* God, I love that accent. Nice to meet you, Lurlene. *(He pinches EVALITA'S butt, she reacts a little too much and squeals.)*

EVALITA. Harmony! *(She spots MAMA WHEELIS glaring at them; quickly.)* Mama Wheelis! *(She goes and hugs her.)*

MAMA WHEELIS. *(less than thrilled)* Hello, Evalita. How's *one* of my grandchildren?

EVALITA. Couldn't be better. *(proudly and loudly)* This is Harmony, Mama Wheelis. Harmony Rhodes.

MAMA WHEELIS. I still ain't deaf, Evalita. Howdy, hippy.

EVALITA. No...it's Harmony. He's a musician in my

band and my fiance. That's his professional name. Harmony Rhodes. His real name was Theodore.

MAMA WHEELIS. *(dry sarcasm)* No wonder he changed
it.

HARMONY. Nice to meet you.

SARA LEE. Well, ya'll sit down...take a load off. *(Everyone
is a little uncomfortable.)*

MAMA WHEELIS. Ya'll want some coffee?

EVALITA. In this heat? No, thanks, Mama Wheelis. But
I could use a beer...if Lurlene don't mind.

LURLENE. *(She does mind, but...)* No, go ahead.

EVALITA. God, Texas is hot. *(Stands in front of the air conditioner and stretches her tube top so air blows on her breasts;
everyone reacts.)*

MAMA WHEELIS. Well, we don't have no beer...so that
nips that in the bud. How 'bout some ice tea?

EVALITA. *(Sits by HARMONY.)* It'll have ta do.

MAMA WHEELIS. *(To HARMONY.)* What about yew?

HARMONY. No, thanks...caffeine's not my cup of tea.
(He laughs at his own joke.)

EVALITA. Cup a tea...oh that's funny. *(No one else seems to
think so.)* Sorry we're late, but we ran into Clarence Hopkins on the way in and I jest had to stop and say
hello.

SARA LEE. *(Shows her engagement ring to EVALITA.)*
We're engaged.

EVALITA. *(looking at ring)* That's funny. Clarence didn't
say a thang about it.

SARA LEE. We picked it out together.

EVALITA. Clarence always was a little cheap.

LURLENE. I think it's beautiful, Sara Lee.

EVALITA. He's still the cutest damn thang in Texas.

SARA LEE. And he knows it too.

EVALITA. He was workin' on a stalled car out by Bluebell's.

(MAMA WHEELIS Enters with the iced tea.)

EVALITA. He had the tightest pair of Levis on and no shirt. Girl, I got a hot flash jest lookin' at that tattooed chest and that sexy ass a his.

MAMA WHEELIS. Trash mouth.

EVALITA. *(taking tea)* Thanks.

MAMA WHEELIS. *(To SARA LEE as she gives her a look.)* I'm gonna go check on my roast.

HARMONY. *(Shakes his head.)* Meat eaters.

LURLENE. I'll help. *(LURLENE and MAMA WHEELIS Exit to the kitchen.)*

MAMA WHEELIS. *(On her way out.)* Nice meetin' ya, Hominy. *(Loud enough for everyone to hear as she and LURLENE Exit.)* I don't thank Evalita's wearin' a brassiere.

SARA LEE. *(Quickly; trying to cover.)* Well, yew better keep yure eyes off Clarence and to yureself, Evalita.

EVALITA. *(looking around)* Well, here we are. Together again. Jest like old times. I cain't hardly stand it.

SARA LEE. Same here. I was jest tellin' Lurlene the same thang. I cain't hardly stand it. Listen, why don't we jest catch up. I'm jest dyin' ta hear about you and yure life and...ever'thang.

EVALITA. And I'm jest bustin' a gut ta tell ya. You ain't

gonna believe this, Sara Lee. I, Evalita Turnover, have become a country and western sanger...with a pop influence.

SARA LEE. You've...become a sanger? Ain't that somethin'.

EVALITA. I'm sort of a cross between Tammy Wynette and Tina Turner. It all happened when one day about two weeks ago Harmony and me was drivin' along, sangin' to the radio—"Me and Bobby McGee" by Janis Joplin, and it hit us. So we started "The Evalita Turnover Band"—Harmony let me pick the name and the rest is hist'ry. And...git this. We jest cut a record. *(Gets too excited.)* I'm gonna be a star, Sara Lee.

SARA LEE. *(Not knowing what to say.)* Ain't that somethin'. *(calling out)* Lurlene, Mama Wheelis, ya'll come quick. Evalita's cut a record.

(LURLENE Enters from kitchen; followed by MAMA WHEELIS.)

LURLENE. *You* cut a record? Singing? *(false enthusiasm)* How exciting.

MAMA WHEELIS. And I jest went to Hollywood and made a new movie with Bette Davis.

EVALITA. Are you callin' me a liar, Mama Wheelis?

MAMA WHEELIS. *(prove it)* Let's hear it.

EVALITA. Well, it's not quite ready yet. It's still gotta be mixed...just as soon as we git the money.

MAMA WHEELIS. She cain't carry a tune in a bucket.

SARA LEE. Well, now girl—yure gonna have ta explain this mixin' business to the country folks.

EVALITA. Harmony's the expert on the business. Yew tell them, dumplin'.

HARMONY. I'd love to. *(She stands and gives him a long passionate kiss.)*

MAMA WHEELIS. Lord! I hope I don't have ta go and git my garden hose.

HARMONY. *(Breaking the kiss.)* Well, mixing a record means taking various instrumental tracks along with the vocal track and making your final product as you hear it on the radio, textured with just the right amount of each.

MAMA WHEELIS. Well, now ain't that jest as clear as a bell.

LURLENE. When it's finished, please send me a copy. I'd love to hear it.

MAMA WHEELIS. *(Under her breath.)* I wouldn't. *(SARA LEE shoots her a look.)*

EVALITA. Quite frankly, Lurlene. It prob'ly ain't yure kinda music. It ain't that Jesus stuff.

LURLENE. Excuse me, Evalita...but my musical tastes are a little more eclectic than just that "Jesus stuff."

MAMA WHEELIS. Lurlene sangs better than yew do, Evalita.

SARA LEE. Mama Wheelis...

MAMA WHEELIS. *(continuing)* She used to sang all them Patsy Cline songs down at the Elks Fraternal Hall. Ray Harper's brother Claude from Nashville heard 'er and sed he could git 'er on the Grand ol' Opery. But Buford wouldn't hear to it.

LURLENE. I was only sixteen, and it wasn't the Lord's will for my life. *(EVALITA is not enjoying this story.)*

MAMA WHEELIS. I bet yew coulda been as big as Loretta
Lynn. Yew have a right perty sangin' voice. Yew sang better'n Evalita. But Buford wouldn't hear to it.

EVALITA. We've heard this story all our lives.

MAMA WHEELIS. I thought yew might need to hear it
again.

EVALITA. Well, I don't. How's Daddy, Sara Lee?

SARA LEE. He ain't good, Evalita. The doctor sed that
stroke could be the beginnin' to the end.

EVALITA. Well, I hope he goes fast if he's sufferin'.
(SARA LEE and LURLENE exchange looks.)

MAMA WHEELIS. *(Under her breath.)* I'll bet yew do.

SARA LEE. *(quickly)* Well, I don't want 'im ta suffer
neither.

HARMONY. *(suddenly)* I'm a little hungry. I'm going to
go out to the truck and get some rice cakes. Anyone
else?

SARA LEE. Sit down, Harmony. Mama Wheelis made a
angel food cake today that'll jest melt in yure mouth.
Mama Wheelis, would yew brang Harmony some of yure
cake?

HARMONY. Did you sweeten that with honey or sugar?

SARA LEE. What difference does it make? I guarantee
ya that yew'll like Mama Wheelis' angel food cake.

MAMA WHEELIS. *(starting for the kitchen)* Durn tootin'.

EVALITA. Harmony's kinda picky about what he
eats.

MAMA WHEELIS. Oh, Lord, would yew listen to that
nonsense?

HARMONY. I eat only natural foods.

MAMA WHEELIS. Well, honey...why don't ya go outside

in the back pasture and graze. That's natural.

SARA LEE. Mama Wheelis!

MAMA WHEELIS. *(As she storms out.)* I see yure still pickin' losers, Evalita. *(LURLENE goes after her.)*

LURLENE. *(from kitchen)* Mama Wheelis, now you've got to learn not to get so worked up. It's not good for your blood pressure.

HARMONY. *(overlapping)* I didn't mean to offend her.

SARA LEE. Don't worry about it, Harmony. I'm sorry, Evalita.

EVALITA. Don't worry about it, Sara Lee. I got used to that kinda treatment a long time ago. *(Changing the subject.)* I'm so glad yew ain't gonna end up a old maid. When's the weddin' date?

SARA LEE. We hadn't set one yet. With Daddy and all...I'm jest waitin' to see if Clarence stays faithful. Yew know he's got that wanderin' eye and wanderin' hands and wanderin' ever'thang else problem.

EVALITA. I know.

SARA LEE. What do yew mean by that?

EVALITA. Jest that I know, Sara Lee. Ever'body in Lowake knows about Clarence Hopkins.

SARA LEE. Well, it jest sounded like when yew sed, "I know" that yew really knew.

EVALITA. Sara Lee, I didn't mean it like that. Shoot, girl, I'm a one man woman... *(SARA LEE gives her a look.)* ...one man at a time, that is. *(They laugh.)*

HARMONY. I'm going to get my rice cakes and go for a walk. Can I bring anything back?

SARA LEE. Naw, Harmony. I thank we're doin' alright. Thanks, enyway.

EVALITA. *(Kissing him goodbye.)* Bye, bye, honey dumplin'.

HARMONY. *(baby talk)* Bye, bye, sweet cheeks.

EVALITA. He don't mean my face. *(She laughs; HARMONY Exits.)*

SARA LEE. I bet he don't. Evalita, I don't mean ta git personal...but where in the hell did yew find this one?

EVALITA. Sara Lee, it was a miracle straight from God. Right after me and Roger busted up...

SARA LEE. Roger?

EVALITA. Yeah, he was the bronco buster I lived with for awhile after me and Abdul got divorced. Yew didn't know 'im. Enyway, he was a nut. Shoulda been committed to a padded room up at Big Sprangs if yew ask me. He beat me up and threw me outta the trailer house. I had nothin' to my name but the clothes on my back and a buck fifty. Told me to git gone or he'd kill me.

SARA LEE. Lord!

EVALITA. So, I started hitch hikin'...

SARA LEE. Yew started hitch hikin'?

EVALITA. Sara Lee, I was desperate. But now I know that it was God's will for my life 'cause if Roger hadn'ta kicked me out, I wouldn'ta been hitch hikin' and Harmony wouldn'ta picked me up. And Harmony was sent by God.

SARA LEE. *(laughs)* Now that's jest about the silliest thang I ever heard. Evalita, yew could take that theory from husband one to husband six, but somehow, I jest don't thank that it was God's will for yew to have been married to six men before yew was forty and for yew to end up with some hippy fella named Harmony.

EVALITA. And when did yew become the assistant to Jesus Christ himself to know *His* will for my life?

SARA LEE. Evalita, I didn't mean nothin' by that. I jest thank that sometimes that people use them words, "God's will" kinda loosely.

EVALITA. Oh, then I guess that what yure sayin' is that yure jest a little more in tune with our Heavenly Father than I am.

SARA LEE. I didn't say that, Evalita. I have been goin' to church a little more regular and last week Reverend Tuttle preached a real good sermon on "The Use and Abuse of God's Will."

(LURLENE and MAMA WHEELIS come to the kitchen door, interested in this conversation.)

EVALITA. Well, la ta da—Sara Lee's been goin' to church, so now she's an expert on the "Use and Abuse of God's Will" 'cause she heard ol' fat ass Rev. Tuttle...who by the way once had an affair with Mildred Keifner, our illustriust soloist...preach one of his borin' ol' sermons.

SARA LEE. Whoa...now yew jest wait one minute, Missy. That was never proved.

EVALITA. No, I won't wait a minute. *Goddamnit,* Sara Lee, ever time I...

MAMA WHEELIS. *(Making a full entrance, followed by LURLENE.)* Now jest hold on, Evalita. The Lord's name is sacred in this house...

LURLENE. Please, let's just try to get along.

EVALITA. That's right. All of ya. Jest gang up on me.

Some thangs never change.

LURLENE. We are not ganging up on yew, Evalita.

MAMA WHEELIS. No, we jest all agree that the Lord's name is not to be taken in vain in this house.

EVALITA. Wake up and smell the coffee, Mama Wheelis. This is 1986.

LURLENE. The Lord's name is the same yesterday, today and forever...

MAMA WHEELIS. Amen!

SARA LEE. That affair was never proved. It was jest gossip.

EVALITA. This has nothin' to do with me sayin' "goddamn!"

LURLENE. That's enough, Evalita.

SARA LEE. For cryin' out loud, let's jest stop...

EVALITA. Yew ain't Mama, Lurlene.

LURLENE. I didn't say I was.

MAMA WHEELIS. I will not have that kinda talk in this house...

EVALITA. Fine. Then I'm leavin'. I need a drank enyway.

SARA LEE. Evalita, please.

LURLENE. We all love you, Evalita. We really do.

EVALITA. Bullshit! *(To LURLENE.)* Bullshit! *(To SARA LEE.)* Bullshit! *(To MAMA WHEELIS.)* Bullshit! Ya'll don't love me...

LURLENE. Stop it, right now, Evalita! I mean it!

EVALITA. Quit actin' like yure mama. Goddamnit. I hate it when yew do that!

MAMA WHEELIS. Where's my razor strap?

SARA LEE. Oh, Lord.

EVALITA. Whatcha gonna do, Mama Wheelis? Whoop me? I'm thirty-three years old, Mama Wheelis...

SARA LEE. No, yure thirty-five. I'm thirty six, Orville's thirty-eight, Lurlene's forty-two, so that makes yew...

EVALITA. Okay! I'm thirty-five. So, I lie too! I cuss, I lie, I cheat—sometimes I even steal ashtrays from motel rooms where I commit adultery! But let me tell ya somethin'. I also live. Daddy ain't the only one dyin' around here. Correction. Daddy's dyin'. Ya'll are dead! Goodbye! Enjoyed this little fam'ly git together! *(She storms out the front door; LURLENE, SARA LEE, and MAMA WHEELIS stand in shock.)*

LURLENE. *(finally)* Well...

SARA LEE. She'll be back.

MAMA WHEELIS. Well, I tell ya one thang. I shore ain't dead! *(She pinches LURLENE and SARA LEE.)*

SARA LEE and LURLENE. Ouch!!!

MAMA WHEELIS. And ya'll ain't neither!

BLACKOUT

Scene 2

About an hour later...the phone is ringing on an empty stage.

SARA LEE. *(O.S.)* Lurlene...Mama Wheelis. Will one of ya'll git that? I'm fixin' up Daddy's room.

(MAMA WHEELIS comes from the kitchen, wiping her hands on a cup towel.)

MAMA WHEELIS. Lurlene, don't let that gravy burn, baby. *(answers phone)* Hello. *(pause)* Why hello, May-belline. *(pause)* I'm fine, jest fine. Jest gittin' ready fer all the kinfolk. Got me a real perty roast down at the Pig. How're yew, honey? *(pause)* Yeah, they're all comin' in. Evalita and Lurlene are done here. Orville and Buford should be here eny minute. Evalita brought a hippy with 'er. I don't know if they're married or not. Drove up in a panel truck. I went out and looked in it. Has a double bed in back and it's real nasty. I swear, Evalita lives like the Winklers. Flittin from man ta man. Trash. Pure dee white trash. I hate ta thank we're kin. *(pause)* Name's Hominy or somethin' queer. *(pause)* No ma'am...why he's so ugly—Jack's butt would make him a Sundey face. Long, scraggly hair, stickin' out ever' which way. Yew know what the Bible sez about that. It's in Corinthians...first or second...I cain't remember which one. Waltzed in here barefooted and I ain't never seen feet that big. *(pause)* Jest a minute. *(calling out)* Sara Lee, it's fer yew. It's Maybelline Cartwright.

SARA LEE. *(O.S.)* Tell 'er I'll call 'er back after'n I finish fixin' up Daddy's room.

MAMA WHEELIS. *(in phone)* She'll call ya back, honey. Tell Liddy Bell and Bo Bob hello.

(HARMONY walks in the front door, carrying a package of rice cakes and his guitar.)

MAMA WHEELIS. *(whispering)* I gotta go. Evalita's hippy

jest walked in.

HARMONY. Hello, Mama Wheelis.

MAMA WHEELIS. Yew can call me, Mrs. Wheelis. I hadn't taken to one of Evalita's husbands since Jack. Ya'll are married, ain't ya?

HARMONY. No, Mrs. Wheelis. We plan to do that when we pass through Las Vegas.

MAMA WHEELIS. *(going to kitchen)* Excuse me. *(calling out)* Lurlene, are yew stirin' that gravy?

LURLENE. *(O.S. from kitchen)* I turned the light out, Mama Wheelis. It's ready.

MAMA WHEELIS. Thanks, baby. *(To HARMONY.)* I took a gander inside that panel truck and there ain't but one double bed in the back. Do yew and Evalita sleep together?

HARMONY. Yeah, Mrs. Wheelis, we do. We are two consenting adults.

MAMA WHEELIS. *(Starts exiting to kitchen.)* Sodom and Gomorroh!

HARMONY. Mrs. Wheelis...I am a person just like you. And right now I'm getting the vibes that you don't like me very much because of what I am...but I like you because of who you are. You think about that, okay?

MAMA WHEELIS. I would if I knew what in the tarnation yew jest sed.

(She Exits; HARMONY looks around the room and SARA LEE Enters from the hallway.)

SARA LEE. I don't know what's keepin' Daddy and Orville. Hello, Harmony. Did yew see Evalita?

HARMONY. No...I did see some farm animals, though.

SARA LEE. That's nice. Well, Evalita got mad at all of us and stormed out. Wonder where she went?

HARMONY. I wouldn't worry. She'll be back. She does that to me all the time.

SARA LEE. That's exactly what I told Mama Wheelis and Lurlene. I'm gonna go finish fixin' Daddy's room. Do me a favor. Holler at me if yew hear 'em drive up.

HARMONY. No sweat.

SARA LEE. Thanks. *(She Exits.)*

HARMONY. *(Walks over and finds a hymnal on the piano, looks through it, finds a song, and starts to sing and play his guitar...slowly, unsure at first.)* "O they tell me of a home far beyond the skies, O they tell me of a home far away."

(LURLENE and MAMA WHEELIS come to the kitchen door. They talk as HARMONY continues to sing.)

MAMA WHEELIS. Well, heaven's to Betsy. That hippy's sangin', "Uncloudy Day." *(They hesitantly start singing with him.)*

HARMONY, LURLENE and MAMA WHEELIS. *(HARMONY motions them over.)* "O they tell me of a home where no storm clouds rise, O they tell me of an uncloudy day." *(LURLENE sits at the piano, playing along with HARMONY. LURLENE and HARMONY pick up the pace on the chorus; MAMA WHEELIS starts clapping.)* "O the land of cloudless day, O the land of an uncloudy day, O they tell me of a home where no storm clouds rise, Oh, they tell me of an uncloudy day."

HARMONY. Take it, Mrs. Wheelis!

MAMA WHEELIS. *(surprised; then)* "O they tell me that He smiles on his children there, And His smile drives their sorrow all away."

(SARA LEE Enters, MAMA WHEELIS motions her over, and she joins MAMA WHEELIS, taking the alto part.)

MAMA WHEELIS and SARA LEE. "And they tell me that no tears ever come again, In that lovely land of uncloudy day."

HARMONY. Everybody now...

ALL. "O the land of cloudless day, O the land of an uncloudy day; O they tell me of a home where no storm clouds rise, O they tell me of an uncloudy day." *(They end to a big finish, all out of breath.)*

MAMA WHEELIS. Oooh wee. I hadn't sang that song since Sid Cranford used to lead them Singspirations down at the church.

HARMONY. That brings back lots of memories. My grandmother from Alabama used to sing that song to me when I was a kid. Meemaw Rhodes.

LURLENE. So you were raised in a Christian home.

HARMONY. Oh, yeah, Daddy would beat the hell out of us kids on the weekdays, get drunk on Saturday nights and screw anything in a skirt. Then on Sunday we'd all go to church.

LURLENE. Well, my oh my.

MAMA WHEELIS. *(Walks over to HARMONY and pats him on the back.)* I've been there, honey. Buster Daddy used to beat me and my younguns somethin' fierce, but when they was all growd, he tried once too often and I hit 'im over the head with a cast iron skillet full of hot bacon grease—kicked him in his male parts and sent 'em packin' with a double barrel shotgun in his back. Never saw that man again.

HARMONY. I can understand why.

MAMA WHEELIS. Buster was mean as a snake. Killed a man onced.

LURLENE. *(To HARMONY.)* Well, you seemed to have turned out alright despite it all.

(SARA LEE and MAMA WHEELIS give her a look; a horn honks outside and SARA LEE and LURLENE go to the window.)

MAMA WHEELIS. Is that Buford and Orville?

SARA LEE. Yes, ma'am, it is.

LURLENE. *(getting choked up)* I hope Daddy's alright.

SARA LEE. Evalita's back. *(Looking up in prayer.)* Oh, God, help us to all act like human bein's. *(She Exits out the front door.)*

LURLENE. Yes, Lord.

MAMA WHEELIS. Amen!

HARMONY. Kum ba ya!

LURLENE. Thy will be done, Lord.

MAMA WHEELIS. His will ain't been done in this fam'ly fer years.

(EVALITA bursts through the door, followed by the troup. SARA LEE and ORVILLE help BUFORD. ORVILLE, carrying a case of beer under the other arm, MARLENE carrying all the luggage, overlapping.)

EVALITA. Look what I found jest wanderin' through the wilderness.

ORVILLE. *(Huge circles of sweat are under his arms.)* It's hot as a sick woman out there. *(He sets the beer down, pops one open and downs it.)*

EVALITA. *(Grabs a beer.)* Thank God yew brought beer. I'm parched.

MARLENE. Hello, ever'body. I've lost weight.

BUFORD. She's a redhead, that's why. Yew cain't trust a redhead. *(MARLENE Exits down hallway with luggage.)*

LURLENE. Oh dear. *(Kisses BUFORD.)* Hello, Daddy. It's Lurlene...Sister. *(BUFORD doesn't respond.)* I didn't realize he'd be this bad. *(Goes and kisses ORVILLE.)* Hello, Orville. *(MARLENE Enters; hugs her.)* Hello, Marlene. How's Jimbo?

ORVILLE. Don't ask.

MARLENE. I've lost weight.

BUFORD. She's a hot blooded redhead!

SARA LEE. *(Hugging ORVILLE.)* I didn't even say hello to yew big brother.

ORVILLE. Howdy, Sara Lee.

MARLENE. *(Very loud; almost angry; surprising herself.)* I've lost weight in case ya'll didn't notice.

EVALITA. Well, look behind yew and yew'll find it.

ORVILLE. Nobody gives a rat's ass, Marlene. Now put this beer in the icebox and shutup. *(She does; Exiting to kitchen.)*

MAMA WHEELIS. *(getting up)* Buford, yew hungry? I got roast, gravy, black-eyed peas and cornbread. And peach cobbler fer desert. Clement Barnes give me some fresh peaches from his tree in 'is back yard. *(MARLENE returns and stands in the doorway.)*

ORVILLE. I'm starved. *(Hugs MAMA WHEELIS.)* How are yew, Mama Wheelis?

MAMA WHEELIS. Alive...and healthy as a horse. Orville yure too fat! *(Walks over to MARLENE and hugs her.)* Hello, honey.

MARLENE. Hello, Mama Wheelis. I've lost weight.

MAMA WHEELIS. I can tell. Yew're just as perty as a picture.

ORVILLE. Yeah, she's down to a ton.

BUFORD. *(suddenly)* I'll jest stay away next time. Them redheads are jest too damn temptin'. Who's shuffle is it? *(He dumps the orange slices onto the coffee table and attempts to shuffle them.)*

EVALITA. Daddy, yew hungry? *(He doesn't respond; staring blank-eyed into space.)*

LURLENE. *(starts to cry)* I can't stand this. Oh, God, please help him. *(She Exits down the hallway.)*

ORVILLE. I hope she don't start preachin' this time.

SARA LEE. *(Looks at Evalita.)* It might do us all some good if she does.

EVALITA. Yeah, Orville. Us heathens need the Lord, yew know.

ORVILLE. *I* ain't a heathen, Evalita. Marlene, brang me a beer.

EVALITA. Grab me one while you're at it, honey. *(MARLENE takes their empties and Exits to the kitchen.)*

ORVILLE. Lurlene jest gits on my nerves sometimes...always spoutin' religion and puttin' on aires 'cause she's a school teacher with a college education. Damn it's hot...Marlene, where's...

MARLENE. *(Yelling O.S.)* I'm comin'. *(She Enters with two beers and gives them to ORVILLE and EVALITA.)*

EVALITA. Ever since Mama died she thanks she was left in charge.

SARA LEE. Well, I'd appreciate it if we all worked extre hard at gittin' along.

MARLENE. *(To MAMA WHELLIS.)* I tried ever'thing— but Herbalean's what fin'ly did it.

ORVILLE. Can it, Marlene.

MARLENE. *(Under her breath.)* He's jealous. He's gained, I've lost. And you know how this heat affects fat people...they sweat like pigs...

ORVILLE. Shut up, Marlene...or I'll slap yew cross-eyed.

MAMA WHEELIS. Ya'll quit fussin'. Yew sound like the Ivey sisters.

(LURLENE returns.)

LURLENE. I'm sorry...it just got to me. I'm fine now.

MAMA WHEELIS. *(Hugging her.)* It's alright, baby.

ORVILLE. *(Spotting HARMONY who is sitting on the piano bench.)* What in the hell is that?

BUFORD. I wanna watch wrestlin'. I don't wanna see that damn Robert Young and that asshole fam'ly. Redheads!

MAMA WHEELIS. Bless 'is heart.

EVALITA. *(Going to HARMONY.)* Oh, I'm sorry. Orville, Marlene...this is my finance, Harmony. Harmony Rhodes.

HARMONY. *(Kisses MARLENE'S hand.)* Nice to meet

ya, Marlene.

MARLENE. Likewise I'm sure.

ORVILLE. They git weirder ever' time, Evalita.

HARMONY. *(Shaking ORVILLE'S hand.)* Nice to meet ya, Orville.

ORVILLE. Yeah, right. *(He wipes his hand on his shirt.)*

SARA LEE. Mama Wheelis, I giss we better wash up fer supper.

MAMA WHEELIS. It'll be ready in five minutes. Marlene, why don't yew come hep me set the table.

MARLENE. Okay.

HARMONY. Can I help?

MAMA WHEELIS. I reakon. *(To MARLENE.)* I giss he's clean.

MARLENE. *(As they Exit; to HARMONY.)* I lost a total of sixty-two pounds and Herbalean's what did it.

BUFORD. Yew jest cain't trust redheads.

MARLENE. *(continuing O.S.)* I can have one meal a day, but I cain't eat the cobbler. Too much sugar.

ORVILLE. *(overlapping)* Diarrhea of the mouth.

SARA LEE. I thank we all need to talk.

ORVILLE. *(anxious)* Have yew read the will?

SARA LEE. No, I haven't. But can yew at least wait 'til he's outta the room before yew start divying up the cash. *(MARLENE, HARMONY and MAMA WHEELIS continue to set table, bringing chairs from kitchen, and moving piano bench to table as this scene continues.)*

ORVILLE. He don't know what's goin' on. *(To BUFORD.)* How ya doin', Daddy?

BUFORD. There's chicken shit in the oats.

ORVILLE. See there.

EVALITA. I'll bet he's worth half a million. That oil well. All them cows. Not to mention the land.

SARA LEE. He sold all that out to the Bright's, Evalita.

EVALITA. Then it's in the bank.

LURLENE. Maybe we ought to plan what we can do to help Daddy while he's still alive.

ORVILLE. There's no hope, Lurlene.

BUFORD. Georgie, yure cheatin' agin. I ain't playin' this cotton pickin' game if yew keep cheatin'.

ORVILLE. Told ya.

LURLENE. I meant...why don't we try and make his last days happy, that's all.

BUFORD. Don't lie ta me. That was a four-trey and it makes fifteen.

EVALITA. He looks happy ta me.

SARA LEE. He's playin' dominoes agin.

EVALITA. He's always happy when he's playin' dominoes.

ORVILLE. He's gone over the edge, big time. 'Bout drove me crazy all the way down here. Played three games of dominoes, two of checkers, and got caught havin' an affair with a redhead.

SARA LEE. That was Paulene Cranford, Sid Cranford's first wife. Mama told me Daddy had an affair with her. She was trash. White trailer trash. *(She looks at EVALITA.)*

BUFORD. Orville, I told yew to water them cows...now git to it.

ORVILLE. He's completely outta his gord. Lurlene, here's his medicine. *(He pitches it to her.)* Give 'im somethin' ta make 'im shut up.

SARA LEE. Orville!

EVALITA. Hurry up, Lurlene! He's sufferin'!

LURLENE. *(not happy with this)* I'll take care of him. *(She helps him down the hallway.)* C'mon, Daddy.

BUFORD. Pitch a bail a hay thataway.

ORVILLE. *(indicating)* I'm pitchin', Daddy. I'm pitchin'. *(Grabs a candy orange slice off the coffee table, eats it, something he does throughout the play.)* Lurlene looks like she's chunked up a little.

SARA LEE. Well, we cain't all maintain our high school figures, Orville.

EVALITA. Speak fer yurself, Sara Lee.

ORVILLE. Yeah, Sara Lee. Me and Evalita's maintained our weight. *(He laughs as he pats his stomach and continues to pop orange slices.)*

(MARLENE Enters from the kitchen with plates.)

MARLENE. Well, Herbalean's what did it fer me...and I'm a dealer now...so it'd take no time for all of ya to git back to yure ideal weight.

EVALITA. Well, let us know when yew git there, Marlene.

ORVILLE. I don't believe that we were talkin' to yew, Marlene. Now finish yure work there, and brang me another beer.

EVALITA. Grab me one too, honey, while yure at it. *(MARLENE Exits back into the kitchen.)*

SARA LEE. *(pause; finally)* I already told Lurlene and Evalita, but I talked to Dr. Wetzel today and he told me that Daddy don't have long. *(MARLENE returns with the beers for ORVILLE and EVALITA and Exits back into the kitchen; she and HARMONY continue to Enter and Exit, setting the table.)*

ORVILLE. *(With his mouth full.)* Told me the same thang. Breaks my heart. But they sed he wadn't sufferin'.

EVALITA. *(not meaning it)* That's a relief.

ORVILLE. Where's the will?

SARA LEE. I don't know, Orville. I thank Daddy keeps a copy in his strong box for safe keepin'.

EVALITA. Well, we need to find that will.

ORVILLE. To git Daddy's affairs in order.

SARA LEE. I know. It jest seems so final. I don't know.

EVALITA. *(Takes SARA LEE'S hand; with false sincerity.)* Honey, I know it's hard, but it must be done.

ORVILLE. Yeah, it must be done.

SARA LEE. I know. I talked to Lawyer Pitman this mornin'. I tried to find that strong box and couldn't, so I thought Lawyer Pitman would have a copy. But he sed that Daddy was in his office a week before his stroke and took his will to make some changes. Daddy musta known.

ORVILLE. What kinda changes?

EVALITA. I was readin' an article in "True Confessions" once and it sed that sometimes people can sense when they're gonna die. Don't that give ya the heeby-geebies?

ORVILLE. What kinda changes?

EVALITA. I can take charge, Sara Lee. Yew don't need a college degree to read a will and arrange a funeral.

ORVILLE. *(exploding)* Will somebody answer me? What kinda changes?

SARA LEE. I ain't shore, Orville...but Lawyer Pitman sed Daddy was real mad. Stormed into 'is office, and took his will. Sed he was gonna make some changes, then he'd brang it back fer Lawyer Pitman to look over. But he never brought it back before he had that stroke.

ORVILLE. It was 'cause a Jimbo. *(Glaring at MARLENE as she sets table.)* We had a big fight over Jimbo. *(pause)* I woulda apalagized if I'd known he was gonna have this stroke...I mean. I don't want 'im ta die mad at me.

SARA LEE. I'm sure you don't, Orville.

EVALITA. How is Jimbo, Orville?

SARA LEE. He's in reform school.

ORVILLE. Wa...Marlene spoiled that boy rotten 'til I couldn't do nothin' else with 'im. *(MARLENE suddenly Exits into kitchen.)* Set the back bedroom on fire while smokin' marijuana cigarettes and sniffin' gasoline. I had ta do somethin'.

SARA LEE. Daddy wanted ta raise that boy himself.

ORVILLE. Like he could do better. Look what he raised. *(SARA LEE and EVALITA give him a look.)* I sed that wrong.

SARA LEE. Well, I hope so.

EVALITA. Are yew sure Lawyer Pitman's got his story straight? Why he's sa old he cain't chew clabber. Hell, he was old when I was a kid. I jest don't trust that ol' coot enyway—with them beady little bird eyes.

SARA LEE. Well, I do. He's as spry as a spring chicken. Defended me when I accidently spilled that solution on Ovella Parsons-Wilks head. Beat her hot shot Abilene lawyer hands down.

ORVILLE. I have done peed in my chili. He ain't gonna leave me doodley-squat. Look what he done to Lurlene.

SARA LEE. That was years ago. He's changed all that 'cause him and Lurlene made up and Daddy even went over to Winters to hear J.D. preach a revival. Sed J.D. was a damn good preacher.

(LURLENE Enters, but stops at the doorway.)

EVALITA. They left him high and dry to run that ranch all by himself. He had the right to do what he did.

LURLENE. *(Pretending to Enter.)* Well, he's finally asleep. I thought that dominoe game would never end. *(Thinking about it, then.)* High and dry, huh...Evalita.

EVALITA. Oh, shit! I didn't mean...

LURLENE. Evalita, I know you probably won't understand this, but J.D. and I were called by God to go into the ministry. Daddy was mad and cut us out of his will at the time...I have no idea what it says now, nor do I care. But at least we gave him five years of hard work on that ranch. All you ever gave him was a lot of grief and five or six son-in-laws.

SARA LEE. Lurlene!

EVALITA. Yew are such a fine Christian woman, Lurlene.

LURLENE. Christianity has nothing to do with this, Evalita. Right is right.

SARA LEE. Lurlene, I thought we were gonna try and git along.

LURLENE. We *all* have to try, Sara Lee.

ORVILLE. I'm doin' my part.

(MAMA WHEELIS Enters from kitchen carrying the roast.)

MAMA WHEELIS. Supper's ready.

ORVILLE. And I'm ready. *(Gets up and goes to table.)*

(MARLENE Enters from kitchen carrying black eyed peas; mumbling.)

MARLENE. As usual.

ORVILLE. Can it, Marlene...I heard that. *(MARLENE flinches; ORVILLE sits down and everyone else gets up and starts gathering around the table.)*

HARMONY. I don't eat meat. I'm a vegetarian.

MAMA WHEELIS. Listen to that nonsense.

MARLENE. I never knew enyone who didn't eat meat...except fer Christie Brinkley. I read it in 'er beauty book.

SARA LEE. Ya'll jest sit enywhere. That'll be fine Harmony. *(MARLENE sits by ORVILLE.)* Yew'll jest have to double up on the black-eyed peas. Marlene that's fine. On second thought...why don't yew sit over here by me? Yew git ta sit by Orville all the time. *(She moves by SARA LEE, and on her other side is HARMONY; EVALITA starts to sit on HARMONY'S other side.)*

MAMA WHEELIS. Whoa, Evalita. That's my seat. Yew sit over there. *(EVALITA kisses HARMONY.)* Don't worry ...me and Marlene ain't gonna steal Harmony away from yew.

EVALITA. I ain't worried. *(She moves to the other side of the table.)*

LURLENE. I'll just sit here.

SARA LEE. Lurlene, will yew return thanks?

ORVILLE. Keep it short. I'm starved.

LURLENE. May we pray? *(She takes ORVILLE'S and MAMA WHEELIS' hand, and with a little confusion, the rest follow suit.)* Dear Lord, we come together before thee today to thank thee for thy bounty and thy love.

MAMA WHEELIS. Yes, Lord.

LURLENE. *(continuing)* We ask that as you draw this family together, that each one of us will realize that love conquers all.

MAMA WHEELIS. Yes, Lord.

LURLENE. *(continuing)* I love my family, Lord, and I ask that you will take greed out of this family and replace it with love.

EVALITA. *(Rolls her eyes.)* Oh, Lord. *(SARA LEE shoots her a look; she quickly goes into MAMA WHEELIS' routine.)* Oh, yes, oh Lord.

LURLENE. *(continuing)* We believe in miracles, Lord, and we ask that Daddy recover from his stroke and that...

BUFORD. *(O.S.)* Georgie. Georgie!

(BUFORD appears at the hallway entrance in his boxer shorts.)

BUFORD. It's that redhead. Git 'er outta my bed!!!

BLACKOUT

Scene 3

AT RISE: The next morning...the phone is ringing as the LIGHTS come up. MAMA WHEELIS is in the kitchen, cooking breakfast. HARMONY and BUFORD are playing checkers in the living room, HARMONY eating a rice cake. HAR-MONY occasionally gets up and stares out the window.

MAMA WHEELIS. *(from kitchen)* Grab that, Hominy, would ya? I'm fixin' breakfast.

BUFORD. Yure move, Georgie.

HARMONY. I'll be right back, Buford. *(He goes to answer the phone.)*

MARLENE. *(O.S.; yelling)* Mama Wheelis...where do yew keep the toilet paper?

HARMONY. *(answering phone)* Hello.

MAMA WHEELIS. *(from kitchen)* It's in the hall closet, honey. On the shelf under the towels.

BUFORD. *(overlapping)* Hurry the hell up, would ya? I ain't got all day.

HARMONY. Evalita, where are you?

BUFORD. Linnie Sue, Orville's diaper's dirty.

HARMONY. This is Harmony. Are you drunk again?

BUFORD. This is gittin' old, Georgie.

HARMONY. Where are you? I've been worried about you.

MAMA WHEELIS. *(Coming out of the kitchen.)* Who is that? *(HARMONY motions for her to wait a second.)* Buford yew hungry?

46

HARMONY. It's Evalita. *(to phone)* Was that a man's voice?

BUFORD. Naw, I jest come from Dot's and had two hamburgers and some french fries. *(MAMA WHEELIS just shakes her head.)*

HARMONY. I heard a man's voice, Evalita. Where are you?

MAMA WHEELIS. Let me talk to her.

BUFORD. Orville's diaper's dirty. I ain't changin' it.

MAMA WHEELIS. *(grabs the phone)* What do yew want?

BUFORD. *(has had enough)* Georgie, are yew gonna shit or wind yure watch?

MAMA WHEELIS. Yure drunk. I can smell liquor on yure breath.

HARMONY. *(Laughs, shakes his head then sits down and moves his checker for Buford.)* Okay, there.

BUFORD. 'Bout time.

MAMA WHEELIS. Listen to me, baby. I don't want yew drankin' enymore. Now yew git someone to drive ya home, right now. Ya hear me? I mean it! Bye, bye.

BUFORD. *(excited)* I got ya now. Crown me.

MAMA WHEELIS. She's drunk. Need's ta go ta AA. Jest like Miss Icy Bright. Fer years was drunk ever' mornin' by seven, but started goin' to them meetin's and is now vice-president of the W.M.U down at the church. I voted fer 'er. I'm tellin' ya, Evalita messed in her nest the day she let Jack go. It's been downhill ever' since. He was the sweetest man. And them babies. Oh, Lord, I cain't even thank about it. I worry all the time about them babies.

BUFORD. Them hamburgers are comin' back on me.

HARMONY. You shouldn't worry. They're great kids
...very well adjusted.

MAMA WHEELIS. Accordin' to who?

HARMONY. According to your standards, Mrs. Wheelis
...and mine.

MAMA WHEELIS. Well, it's a miracle straight from God.
Evalita toted them younguns from one end of the country to the other, flittin' from man ta man.

BUFORD. Linnie Sue, we got eny Rolaids?

MAMA WHEELIS. I'm Lois, Buford. Lois Wheelis...yure
mother-in-law. Linnie Sue is dead. *(She starts to Exit to
the kitchen.)*

BUFORD.. We got eny Rolaids, Lois Wheelis?

MAMA WHEELIS. *(Exiting to kitchen.)* I'll check in the
kitchen. *(Shakes her head.)* Bless 'is heart. *(She talks to HAR-
MONY from the kitchen as she looks for a Rolaid.)* I'm glad Jack
fin'ly won custady. Hear he's got a right perty wife now.
*(She returns carrying a bottle of Milk of Magnesia and a table-
spoon.)* Buford, I couldn't find no Rolaids, but here's
some Milk a Magnesia. *(She gives him a couple of tablespoons.)*
That's right. Now one more. *(She sets the bottle down;
BUFORD picks it up and proceeds to drink the remainder of the
MOM.)* They'll give 'em a good home. Somethin' they
couldn't git livin' like a band a gypsies in a panel
truck.

BUFORD. Dot's makes the best milk shakes.

MAMA WHEELIS. *(Seeing what he has done.)* Oh, my Lord.
Buford has drunk all the Milk a Magnesia. Buford, why'd
yew do that? We're gonna have ta take 'im ta Abilene to
git 'is stomick pumped. Oh, my Lord.

BUFORD. Dot's makes the best milk shakes. I'm gonna

try strawberry next time.

HARMONY. How much was left in the bottle?

MAMA WHEELIS. 'Bout a quarter of it.

HARMONY. Then I don't think there's any reason to worry. *(He is reading the label.)* He'll be alright.

MAMA WHEELIS. What do yew know about it? I'm gonna call Dr. Wetzel. *(She goes for the phone.)*

BUFORD. Yure move, Georgie. Boy, that hit the spot.

HARMONY. I was a pre-med student for three years before I switched to music. He'll have diarreah for awhile, but he'll be just fine. Trust me.

MAMA WHEELIS. *(a little hesitant)* Alright. Shoo-wee, that give me a scere. *(Staring at HARMONY for a second.)* Yew know, if it wadn't fer that crazy hairdo and them earrings, yew might jest be a regular person. Of course, I strongly believe that nobody's in their right mind who shackes up with Evalita.

HARMONY. You may be right.

MAMA WHEELIS. I know I'm right.

BUFORD. Don't mind me. I'll jest sit here and listen while yew two yack. It's yure move, damnit!

HARMONY. Just a second, Buford. *(This is hard; finally.)* Evalita stayed out all night last night. Said she was going to visit some friends. But she never came back. She stayed out all night.

MAMA WHEELIS. Like a cat in heat.

HARMONY. *(This strikes him funny.)* Yew make me laugh, Mrs. Wheelis.

MAMA WHEELIS. Well, I don't mean to.

HARMONY. I know.

BUFORD. *(Trying not to lose his temper.)* One Mississippi,

two Mississippi's...*(He continues to count.)*

MAMA WHEELIS. I wanna apologize for actin' ugly when yew first come.

HARMONY. Mrs. Wheelis...please. Don't worry about it.

MAMA WHEELIS. Yew can call me Mama Wheelis now.

BUFORD. *(Has had enough; He knocks the checker board off the table.)* That's it. I ain't gonna sit here and wait fer yew ta move if yure gonna gab all day. I'm gonna go combine the lower field. *(He walks to closet and gets his hat, turns to MAMA WHEELIS.)* Where's my tractor? *(Puts on his hat and walks straight down the hallway.)*

MAMA WHEELIS. Bless 'is heart. *(She and HARMONY pick up the checkers.)*

ORVILLE. *(O.S.)* Hurry the hell up, Marlene. I'm about to bust my bladder out here.

MARLENE. *(O.S.)* I'll be done in a second.

MAMA WHEELIS. I'm gonna go make sure Buford's alright. *(She starts to Exit.)*

HARMONY. Mama Wheelis.

MAMA WHEELIS. *(turning around)* Huh?

HARMONY. Thanks.

MAMA WHEELIS. Yure welcome, honey. *(She Exits down the hallway.)*

(MARLENE Enters from hallway, passing MAMA WHEELIS.)

MARLENE. Mornin', Mama Wheelis.
MAMA WHEELIS. Mornin', Marlene.

MARLENE. Mornin', Harmony.

HARMONY. Mornin', Marlene. Did you sleep well?

MAMA WHEELIS. I did. And guess what?

HARMONY. This is just out of the blue, but I'll bet you've lost some more weight.

MARLENE. *(squeals)* Yew noticed. One and a quarter more L.B.'s.

ORVILLE. *(O.S.)* Good God, Marlene. Would yew learn ta strike a match. Yew done singed my nose hairs. Damn Herbalean.

MARLENE. *(Yelling back at him; again surprising herself.)* It cleanses my system. *(She Exits, embarrassed, to the kitchen.)*

MAMA WHEELIS. *(Returns, carrying BUFORD'S hat.)* He's sound asleep. Was still wearin' his hat. *(She hangs up the hat and goes into the kitchen.)* I gotta finish gittin' breakfast.

MARLENE. *(Returning with a glass of Herbalean.)* Yew know, I'm on Herbalean. That's how I did it.

HARMONY. I don't think those radical diets are all that good for you. Myself, I eat healthy...all natural...no meat. *(MAMA WHEELIS returns and starts setting the table.)* And I don't drink. *(whispering)* I do smoke a little weed now and then, but that's it.

MARLENE. Yew smoke marijuana cigarettes? *(MAMA WHEELIS reacts.)*

HARMONY. Not often. Just one little vice. But I figure with a good diet, a little pot won't hurt you. Hey, I want you to try something. *(He goes to the table and grabs his rice cakes.)*

MARLENE. I've always wanted to try marijuana cigarettes. *(MAMA WHEELIS reacts and Exits mumbling disapprovals.)* One time I thought I had found some in Jimbo's room, so I rolled it up, and smoked it and got a little dizzy, but nothin' much happened. Then I found a box a catnip on his shelf and I thought, why in the world does this boy have catnip...we don't have a cat. We have a dawg, name's Bimbo...Jimbo's our boy, Bimbo's our dawg. Enyway, it turned out that I had smoked catnip. I coulda killed Jimbo.

HARMONY. Well, we'll have to light up the real stuff later. Here, try this. *(He hands her a rice cake.)*

MARLENE. This ain't on my diet.

HARMONY. Aw, come on. Only 35 calories each.

MARLENE. Okay. *(She crunches into the rice cake.)* Good lord, this tastes like styerfoam.

HARMONY. It's better with unsalted peanut butter and honey.

MARLENE. It'd have ta be. It's like eatin' a ice chest. *(Hands it back to him.)* Here, I don't want it. If I had ta eat them, I'd jest shrivel up and die. That's prob'ly why they call it *diet* food. Herbalean's real tasty.

ORVILLE. *(O.S.)* Lurlene, it's all yures. Marlene stunk it up perty bad, but I opened a winda.

MARLENE. Fat ass! *(She quickly covers her mouth.)*

(MAMA WHEELIS enters from kitchen.)

MAMA WHEELIS. Watch yure mouth.

MARLENE. Sorry, Mama Wheelis. *(MAMA WHEELIS Exits; to HARMONY; whispering.)* It looks like at her age she'd be hard a hearin'.

MAMA WHEELIS. *(Comes to kitchen door.)* I heard that. Ya'll wash up. Breakfast is nearly ready.

(ORVILLE Enters from hallway.)

ORVILLE. I'm as hungry as a bear.

MARLENE. *(To HARMONY.)* And mean as a snake.

ORVILLE. Don't start with me, Marlene. I ain't in the mood.

MARLENE. Yew never are. I dropped one and a quarter more pounds.

ORVILLE. Well, let's all stand up and do a jig.

MARLENE. Jealous. *(Starts to Exit; ORVILLE grabs her.)*

ORVILLE. Woman, don't talk back ta me, or I'll slap the thunder outta yew.

MAMA WHEELIS. *(Comes to the kitchen door; to the rescue.)* Marlene, come hep me in the kitchen. *(Exits back into the kitchen.)*

MARLENE. Okay. *(She tries to get away from ORVILLE, but he bullies her up against the wall.)*

ORVILLE. Woman, I don't know what's gotten into yew lately, but don't yew ever talk ta me like that agin.

MARLENE. Take yure hands offa me right now! I am takin' Phil Donahue's advice and standin' up for myself as an equal partner in this marriage. *(He squeezes her arms.)* Ouch, let go of me or I'm gonna start screamin' my head off. Let go of me NOW! *(She stomps his foot.)*

ORVILLE. Ouch!

MAMA WHEELIS. *(Coming to kitchen door; trying to help again.)* Marlene, come hep me scramble these eggs.

MARLENE. I'm comin', Mama Wheelis. *(As she Exits; to ORVILLE.)* I'm warnin' yew, Orville. I'm gittin' *real* tired!

ORVILLE. *(Limps to chair in living room, mumbling, he sits opposite HARMONY.)* Damn crazy woman. *(He picks up a newspaper and starts reading it.)*

HARMONY. *(After a long pause.)* So, Orville...did you sleep well?

ORVILLE. What? Yeah, fine, jest fine.

HARMONY. Anything interesting in there?

ORVILLE. *(Giving HARMONY a look.)* I'll let yew read it after'n I'm done.

HARMONY. I've already read it.

ORVILLE. Then whey the hell did yew ask me if enythang was interestin' in there?

HARMONY. Just trying to make small talk.

ORVILLE. *(Going back to his reading.)* Well, don't tax yure brain 'cause we don't have ta talk.

MAMA WHEELIS. *(Coming to kitchen door.)* Orville, how many eggs yew want?

ORVILLE. Six...over easy.

MAMA WHEELIS. Thank heavens the chicken's are layin'. Hominy, how 'bout yew?

HARMONY. I'll have a couple scrambled...if you have enough. *(MAMA WHEELIS laughs and Exits; ORVILLE shoots HARMONY a look, HARMONY smiles; after a pause.)* So, Orville...

ORVILLE. *(not thrilled)* What?

HARMONY. What kind of work do you do?

ORVILLE. I work fer the city.

(MARLENE Enters carrying food and putting it on the table.)

MARLENE. He dumps trash.

ORVILLE. Shut up, Marlene.

MARLENE. *(Exiting.)* Jealous.

HARMONY. Oh, so you're a sanitation engineer, so to speak.

ORVILLE. Are yew getting smart with me, boy?

HARMONY. No, not at all.

ORVILLE. Well, fer yure information...it's a damn important job. This country would be a helluva mess without us. On top a that, yew can find some good stuff that yew can keep. It's amazin' what people throw out.

HARMONY. Well, I wasn't making fun. That's what we call them in California...sanitation engineers. They're very well respected.

ORVILLE. Really? Sanitation engineer, huh?

HARMONY. Yeah.

ORVILLE. I kinda like the sound of that. Sanitation engineer. *(ORVILLE is beaming; MARLENE returns with some plates and then Exits back into the kitchen.)* See them earrings Marlene's wearin'?

HARMONY. Yeah. They're nice.

ORVILLE. Found 'em at the dump. Someone jest threw 'em out. I thank they're real pearls too.

HARMONY. They look genuine to me.

ORVILLE. Had to fight ol' Larry Johnson fer 'em. Gave 'em to 'er fer Christmas. Brought tears to 'er eyes.

HARMONY. How thoughtful.

ORVILLE. Sanitation engineer, huh?

(SARA LEE enters from hallway; she is fully dressed, ready to go somewhere.)

SARA LEE. Mornin', Harmony. Mornin', Orville. *(calling out)* Mornin' Mama Wheelis and Marlene.

EVERYONE. Mornin', Sara Lee.

ORVILLE. Hey, Sara Lee...ask me what I do for a livin'.

SARA LEE. What for...I know what yew do fer a livin'...yew dump trash. *(calling out)* Mama Wheelis, don't cook me no breakfast 'cause I gotta go to the bank and look in Daddy's safe deposit box fer the key to his strong box.

(MAMA WHEELIS comes to kitchen door.)

MAMA WHEELIS. Yew should eat breakfast, honey. It's the most important meal of the day. I heard that on the Hollywood Squares.

SARA LEE. Oh, lord.

MAMA WHEELIS. *(Returning to kitchen.)* I'm glad they brought that show back.

ORVILLE. Come on, Sara Lee, ask me what I do fer a livin'?

SARA LEE. Okay, Orville. What do yew do fer a livin'?

ORVILLE. I'm a sanitation engineer. Yew git it? Sanitation engineer.

(MARLENE comes from kitchen with more food.)

MARLENE. We git it, Orville. It means yew dump trash.

ORVILLE. Shut the hell up, Marlene! *(Whispering to HARMONY.)* Don't tell 'er where I got them earrings.

HARMONY. No problem.

MAMA WHEELIS. *(Coming from kitchen, continuing to set table etc.)* Did yew look in on Buford? He was playin' checkers this mornin' with Hominy, then he went to bed.

SARA LEE. He's still sleepin'. He didn't sleep too good last night. Lurlene and me took turns settin' up with 'im. Kept tellin' us he needs ta see his will. Do yew know where his strong box is? I cain't find it.

ORVILLE. Did he say enythang about me, Sara Lee?

SARA LEE. No, Orville. Is Evalita still asleep? Harmony, I wish that ya'll woulda stayed in the house last night. We coulda pulled out this here sofa bed. And Evalita coulda helped with Daddy.

MAMA WHEELIS. One of 'em coulda slept on that sofa bed and one of 'em coulda slept on a pallet.

(LURLENE Enters from hallway.)

LURLENE. Good mornin', everyone.

EVERYONE. Mornin', Lurlene.

SARA LEE. Well, I better go.

MAMA WHEELIS. Well, I shore hope I didn't cook breakfast and ever'body jest scatters off without a bite. Yure goin' to the bank, Marlene's on that crazy diet, Evalita's out alley cattin' and my hippy friend's eatin' rice patties. Lurlene, yew hungry?

LURLENE. Yes ma'am.

SARA LEE. What'dya mean, "Evalita's out alley cattin'?"

MAMA WHEELIS. She stayed out all night. That's what Hominy sed. She called this mornin' drunk as a skunk.

LURLENE. Never a dull moment.

MAMA WHEELIS. Honey, the bank don't open 'til ten. I made grits, bacon, gravy, bisquits and eggs.

LURLENE. I swear, it looks like after five husbands and no tellin' how many in between, she would have had enough by now.

SARA LEE. Well, maybe we shouldn't jump to conclusions.

LURLENE. Oh, come on, Sara Lee. She stayed out all last night while we were sitting up with Daddy. It doesn't take an Einstein to know what she did.

SARA LEE. Well, she is an adult, so I guess that this doesn't concern us. And yew know what the Bible sez, Lurlene, "Judge not that ye be not judged."

LURLENE. *(caught; embarrassed)* Right. *(changing subject)* Mama Wheelis, could I help you with breakfast? *(HARMONY gets up and starts for the front door.)*

MAMA WHEELIS. It's all ready, honey. Yew could take Buford's tray to 'im. See if he'll eat.

LURLENE. *(Going to kitchen.)* I'd be happy to.

MAMA WHEELIS. *(To SARA LEE.)* Breakfast is the most important meal of the day. Now who was that who sed that on the Hollywood Squares?

SARA LEE. Okay, I'll eat breakfast.

(The front door slams and we see HARMONY through the window walking away.)

SARA LEE. Shit.

MAMA WHEELIS. Watch yure mouth.

SARA LEE. I'm sorry, Mama Wheelis. *(continuing)*

Lurlene, Harmony jest walked out the front door. Yew sed that stuff about Evalita right in front of him.

LURLENE. *(Coming to doorway.)* Oh, dear. I didn't even think.

ORVILLE. Damn hippy queer. Serves 'im right.

MARLENE. I thank that Harmony is a very nice person and we should try to treat him like fam'ly.

ORVILLE. Fam'ly? Woman, yure outta yure mind. He's a hippy, prob'ly a bisexul homo and he looks like he's from outer space. *(LURLENE goes back in kitchen.)*

MARLENE. Well, I thank he's real nice.

ORVILLE. Horseshit...he's a damn hippy pinko communist...

MAMA WHEELIS. Young man, I've had jest about enough of yew.

ORVILLE. But I was jest...

MAMA WHEELIS. Don't talk back ta me. I'm gittin' sick and tired of yure mouth. Yew may be big, but yew ain't too big fer me to git my razor strap after yew. *(MARLENE starts laughing; LURLENE returns from kitchen with tray.)*

ORVILLE. What the hell yew laughin' at?

MAMA WHEELIS. Stop it! Now! There is a man that is sick in this house. He may even be dyin'. *(She chokes up but remains strong and angry.)* And yew don't give a plug nickel about 'im. Well, I do. He's very dear to my heart. So, shut up...all of yew. Behave. Yure gittin' on my nerves. Now sit down...ever' last one of yew. Yure gonna eat breakfast whether yew like it or not. *(Everyone obeys except LURLENE.)*

LURLENE. *(Exiting down hall with tray.)* I'll just take this tray to Daddy and give him his medicine, then I'll be right back to eat my breakfast.

MAMA WHEELIS. Thank you, Lurlene. She is so sweet. Bless 'er heart—I believe that if she hadn't been a preacher's wife that she'da made a nurse. She reminds me so much of Linnie Sue. Orville, return thanks.

ORVILLE. *(in disbelief)* Mama Wheelis, I ain't prayed in years.

MAMA WHEELIS. Then it's high time yew start.

ORVILLE. *(Awkwardly looks around as everyone bows their head; finally.)* God is great, God is good, and we thank him for our food, and please be with Daddy, Amen. Marlene, pass the bisquits.

MAMA WHEELIS. Pore ol' Buford. who'd a thought. He was always healthy as a horse.

ORVILLE. And the bacon.

SARA LEE. That jest goes to show ya. Yew never know.

MARLENE. Yeah, fat people drop dead all the time with heart attacks.

ORVILLE. *(between bites)* Shut up, Marlene and pass the salt.

SARA LEE. He could git well. But Dr. Wetzel sed that there wadn't no hope. That we'd jest have to keep 'im and watch 'im die.

ORVILLE. *(between bites)* It's a cryin' shame.

SARA LEE. I wonder what ever happened to miracles. They're plastered all over the Bible. Sometimes I thank God has gotten hard a hearin'.

MAMA WHEELIS. Sara Lee!

SARA LEE. I mean it. Yew been prayin' fer Daddy, I been prayin' fer Daddy...we all know that Lurlene's been prayin' fer Daddy.

ORVILLE. Pass the butter, please.

SARA LEE. *(joking)* Of course, we all jest witnessed Orville's first prayer ever.

ORVILLE. That ain't true. *(mouth full)* I prayed a bunch when I was a kid.

MARLENE. Maybe God got mad when Orville stopped praying.

ORVILLE. Don't blame this on me. Pass the grits, please.

SARA LEE. I jest thank God got hard a hearin'.

(A horn honks outside.)

MAMA WHEELIS. *(getting up)* Now who in the world could that be? *(To SARA LEE.)* Young lady, yew better watch how yew talk 'bout God. Lot's wife turned ta stone.

ORVILLE. *(belches)* Good breakfast, Mama Wheelis.

MAMA WHEELIS. Thank ya, honey. *(Looks out window.)* Sara Lee, that's Clarence. Yew go tell him that horn honkin' is fer callin' the cows. *(SARA LEE gets up.)* Oh my lord, Evalita's gittin out of his pickup staggerin' drunk.

SARA LEE. What? *(She rushes to window.)*

(LURLENE is running to the hallway door screaming to the top of her lungs.)

LURLENE. Ya'll come quick! Daddy's heart stopped! I think he's dead! *(Everyone reacts, and:)*

BLACKOUT

ACT TWO
Scene 1

AT RISE: Later that afternoon...the PHONE is ringing as the LIGHTS come up. BUFORD is watching an invisible television by himself in the living room. The PHONE continues to ring.

BUFORD. Come on, Tiny Timmy. Body slam the son-of-a-bitch. *(He goes over to the phone, picks it up and slams it back down.)* Linnie Sue, brang me a beer, please. *(upset)* Aw, come on, ref, are yew blind? *(calling out)* That was Liddy Bell Cartwright. Sed the Daughters' meetin's been cancelled 'cause of the snow. *(Looking back to set.)* Oh, he's mad now. Kill 'im Timmy. Yew got 'im now. That's my boy. *(calling out)* Honey, we'll watch Bonanza after this. It's almost over. *(suddenly excited)* That's it, yew got 'im. One, two, three.

(BUFORD is jumping, whooping it up as SARA LEE and LURLENE walk in the front door, drenched with sweat. They walk over and stand in front of the air conditioner, watching BUFORD.)

BUFORD. Yew did it! Tiny Timmy wins again! That's my boy. *(Letting out a loud holler.)* Yeee—hi!!!

SARA LEE. He's watchin' midget wrastlin'. He fergits I

63

moved his T.V. to his bedroom.

BUFORD. Sister...turn that T.V. off, would ya?

LURLENE. *(Looks at SARA LEE.)* Sure, Daddy. *(She pretends to turn it off.)* Did yew enjoy your wrastlin'?

BUFORD. Yeah, Sawed-Off Sam jest got 'is butt whupped by Tiny Timmy.

LURLENE. That's nice.

BUFORD. Yeah, that Timmy's tough. Is it still snowing outside?

SARA LEE. *(Looks at LURLENE questioning.)* No, Daddy, it stopped.

BUFORD. I'm cold. Where's my sweater?

LURLENE. You're wearing it, Daddy.

BUFORD. Yew girls better change into your play clothes and help yure mama with supper.

LURLENE. Daddy...do yew need anything?

BUFORD. Naw, Linnie Sue's brangin' me a beer. How was school?

SARA LEE. We had ta go to the bank, Daddy...remember? Where's Evalita and Orville? They sed they would take care of yew while we was gone.

BUFORD. I can take care of myself. *(suddenly getting angry)* I can take care of myself!

LURLENE. We know you can. Where are Evalita and Orville, Daddy?

BUFORD. I sent 'em down to Lawyer Pitman's to git a copy of my will. I wanna talk to ya'll about it.

SARA LEE. Daddy, Lawyer Pitman sed he didn't have the will. Sed yew took it and changed it a coupla weeks ago. Do yew remember that?

BUFORD. I remember I told yew girls to help yure

mama with supper and yew didn't do it. I oughta take my belt ta both of ya.

LURLENE. Oh, Daddy. *(BUFORD stares blank-eyed.)*

SARA LEE. Daddy, are yew alright?

BUFORD. *(after a while)* Somethin's wrong. I jest ain't myself. I cain't remember what I did with my will. Is Linnie Sue here? I made a mistake.

LURLENE. No, Daddy. She's gone.

BUFORD. Where'd she go?

SARA LEE. *(Not knowing what else to say.)* To the Piggly Wiggly. What mistake did yew make, Daddy? Yew sed yew made a mistake.

BUFORD. Ever'body makes mistakes. I ain't the only one, dad gummit!

LURLENE. Daddy...I made a mistake too. *(This is hard.)* Yew remember when J.D. surrendered to preach and yew cut us out of your will?

BUFORD. J.D. turned out ta be a damn good preacher. Better'n ol' Reverend Tuttle. Who'd thought. Ol' farm boy a preacher. J.D. was like my son, ya know.

LURLENE. I know he was, Daddy.

BUFORD. Orville shouldn'ta put Jimbo in reform school. J.D. woulda raised a good boy. Not a dopehead.

LURLENE. Daddy, we raised two fine boys. J.D. and I raised two fine Christian boys...Randy and Bobby. Remember my boys? You bought them a horse, a Shetland pony. I can't remember it's name. Grasshopper or Katydead or something. *(BUFORD just stares blank-eyed.)*

SARA LEE. He don't remember, Lurlene.

LURLENE. I'm sorry, Daddy. I'm sorry that we didn't try harder to make things right. I'm sorry you don't remember my boys. *(struggling)* We didn't want to leave you, Daddy. Especially so soon after Mama had died. We had to. The Lord was calling us.

BUFORD. Well, I sure as hell never heard 'im.

LURLENE. *(after a while)* Will you forgive me, Daddy? *(no answer)* I don't care about the will. *(Takes his hand.)* Don't worry about the will. I just want you to know how much I love you...and I'm sorry you didn't know that for all those years.

BUFORD. *(remembering; softly)* Crickett. The horse's name was Crickett.

LURLENE. *(Hugs him.)* Oh, Daddy.

BUFORD. *(Tears in his eyes; very coherent.)* I wanted to see them grandbabies grow up. Linnie Sue left and yew always reminded me of Linnie Sue. I didn't want you to leave me, Sister...for enybody. Not even for Jesus. *(They hug.)*

(EVALITA and ORVILLE walk in the front door.)

EVALITA. Lawyer Pitman's senile. He don't know shit from shinola.

ORVILLE. We gotta find that thang.

BUFORD. *(suddenly)* Orville, Lita...I wanna talk to ya'll. I wanna talk to all my kids. Where's Sarie Lee?

SARA LEE. I'm here, Daddy.

EVALITA. *(Rushes to him, followed by ORVILLE.)* We're all here, Daddy.

ORVILLE. Yeah, Daddy, we're all here. *(counting heads)*

One, two, three, four.

BUFORD. Sit down, all of ya.

SARA LEE. Are yew alright, Daddy?

BUFORD. No. I've had a stroke and I'm goin' crazy.

LURLENE. It's alright, Daddy.

BUFORD. I cain't remember where I put my will.

EVALITA. Is it in your strong box, Daddy?

BUFORD. I cain't remember.

EVALITA. Now thank real hard, Daddy. It'll come ta ya.

BUFORD. I cain't thank. It's somewhere though.

ORVILLE. Well, that puts my mind at ease.

BUFORD. Somewhere around the house...I thank. I made a mistake. I gotta fix the mistake.

ORVILLE. He cut me out. I jest know it. I done peed in my chili. I could kill Jimbo.

EVALITA. Aw, hush up yure bawlin'. We're all up shit creek if we cain't find the damn thang. Does enybody know the law?

BUFORD. I want ya'll to know somethin'. I want yew all to know...tha...(He starts to cry.) ...that I love yew...ever' last one of yew.

SARA LEE. (crying) We love yew too, Daddy.

LURLENE. We do.

EVALITA. All of us do, Daddy.

ORVILLE. Are yew shore yew cain't remember where yew put that will?

SARA LEE. Orville!

BUFORD. I'm real tired. I wanna go ta bed.

LURLENE. I'll take him.

SARA LEE. I'll help yew. (They help him up and start walking *him towards the hallway entrance.)* Easy now.

BUFORD. *(Resisting; walking by himself.)* I can take care of myself. *(SARA LEE follows him; LURLENE stays.)*

LURLENE. *(She stops and turns to ORVILLE and EVALITA.)* I'm sorry I gave everybody such a scare this morning. He was just so quiet and I couldn't find a pulse. I guess I panicked.

ORVILLE. Don't worry about it, Lurlene. *(She Exits; under his breath.)* Bimbo.

EVALITA. Well, let's look for that will. It's gotta be here somewhere.

ORVILLE. Well, I don't see no use. He's mad at me.

EVALITA. Start lookin'. Look ever'where. He sed he couldn't remember if it was in that strongbox. It could be enywhere.

ORVILLE. It don't matter 'cause I done peed in my chili.

EVALITA. Will yew jest shut the hell up about peein' in yure chili and start lookin'? It turns my stomick. *(They start going through everything in the living room; drawers, the piano bench, the closet, basically very quickly making holy havoc of the place.*

ORVILLE. It ain't here.

EVALITA. Look behind them pictures.

ORVILLE. *(mumbling)* I'm lookin', I'm lookin'.

(MAMA WHEELIS Enters the back door of the kitchen, singing a hymn.)

EVALITA. Oh, shit. That's Mama Wheelis. Hurry, put that back. *(ORVILLE panics and in his effort to re-hang the pic-*

*ture, bumps the knick knack shelf, knocking down a cup. It shatters.
the room is now a mess and they desperately try to clean it up.)*
She's gonna kill us.

MAMA WHEELIS. *(Enters when she hears the breakage, wearing gardening attire and carrying some vegetables.)* What in the cat hair is goin' on here?

EVALITA. Oh, shit.

MAMA WHEELIS. Watch yure mouth. Now answer me. What in the cat hair is goin' on here?

EVALITA. Nothin', Mama Wheelis.

(SARA LEE enters from hallway.)

ORVILLE. Nothin', Mama Wheelis.

MAMA WHEELIS. *(Bends over and picks up a piece of the cup.)* Oh my Lord! Yew broke one of Linnie Sue's cups from her collection. Yew oughta be ashamed of yureself.

ORVILLE. I'm sorry, Mama Wheelis.

EVALITA. I'm sorry too, Mama Wheelis. But Orville broke the cup. *(ORVILLE pinches her.)* Ouch, stop it! He pinched me, Mama Wheelis.

SARA LEE. *(laughing)* They're tryin' to find Daddy's will.

EVALITA. To git Daddy's affairs in order.

ORVILLE. To git Daddy's affairs in order, Mama Wheelis.

EVALITA. *(whispering)* Sara Lee, I thought we decided not to leave Lurlene alone with Daddy enymore.

SARA LEE. That was yure idea, Evalita.

MAMA WHEELIS. And what give yew two monkeys the right to git Buford's affairs in order?

EVALITA. We're his children.

ORVILLE. We're his children, Mama Wheelis.

MAMA WHEELIS. *(To ORVILLE.)* Polly Parrot, would yew jest keep quiet if yew don't have nothin' of yure own ta say?

EVALITA. *(Whispering to SARA LEE.)* She's up to no good, Sara Lee.

ORVILLE. Yeah, she's up to no good, Sara Lee. We need ta watch her. But I ain't got a prayer. I done peed in my...

EVALITA. If yew say that one more time...

(LURLENE Enters.)

LURLENE. He's sleeping real sound. I gave him some more medication.

EVALITA. See there.

MAMA WHEELIS. Lurlene, I wish yew'd look at this room. *(To ORVILLE and EVALITA.)* I oughta take my razor strap ta both of ya.

EVALITA. Oh, brother.

SARA LEE. *(On the verge of laughing.)* Orville and Evalita made holy hell outta the livin' room tryin' ta find Daddy's will.

EVALITA. We had ever' right, Mama Wheelis. We are his children.

ORVILLE. Yeah, Mama Wheelis. We are his children.

MAMA WHEELIS. I give up. If yew two had a brain 'tween ya, yew'd be dangerous. *(LURLENE and SARA LEE start to snicker.)* Now I want both of ya to clean this mess up. I don't want to see one thang outta place. And glue

Linnie Sue's cup back together. Ya hear me?

EVALITA. Yes, Mama Wheelis.

ORVILLE. Yes, Mama Wheelis. *(SARA LEE and LUR-LENE are one level above snickering now; EVALITA and ORVILLE attempt to clean the mess.)*

MAMA WHEELIS. Hurry up. And watch those hymnals. I don't want eny pages missing. Oh, Sara Lee. Hep these nitwits, please. *(She throws her hands up and goes to the kitchen to put up her vegetables. LURLENE and SARA LEE are resisting hysteria as ORVILLE and EVALITA frantically try to clean the room.)*

ORVILLE. What the hell ya'll laughin' at, huh?

SARA LEE. Nothin'. *(MAMA WHEELIS re-enters with beans to snap.)*

LURLENE. Nothin' at all. *(She bursts out laughing, full force, followed by SARA LEE, then MAMA WHEELIS gets tickled.)*

MAMA WHEELIS. Well, whatever it was, I musta missed it.

EVALITA. What's so funny? Are ya'll laughin' at us?

LURLENE. *(Barely able to talk through the laughter.)* You two just looked like you were kids getting scolded, that's all. It reminded me of that summer we went to stay with Mama Wheelis, and Orville dropped his little red ball down the hole of the outhouse. *(SARA LEE is hysterical; ORVILLE and EVALITA still stonefaced.)*

MAMA WHEELIS. Oh, Lord.

ORVILLE. I don't thank this is very funny.

EVALITA. I don't neither.

SARA LEE. *(laughing even harder)* Remember, he paid Evalita a dime to crawl down there and git it...

LURLENE. And she got stuck, so Orville, you had to go

dig her out.

ORVILLE. I know the story. I was there.

EVALITA. Me too...it really wadn't that funny.

MAMA WHEELIS. *(Now laughing so hard she is wiping tears from her eyes.)* Lord, I never vomited so hard in all my life. I stood there with the garden hose hosin' both of yew down...neked...both of ya buck neked, covered with doo doo from head to toe. *(EVALITA starts laughing, then ORVILLE follows suit.)*

SARA LEE. Ooh wee, my sides...my sides are achin'.

LURLENE. I used to love to spend summers at Mama Wheelis'.

ORVILLE. Me too. I used to love to kill horny toads with my Bee-Bee gun.

SARA LEE. Yeah, that was always a real perty sight.

LURLENE. Those were the good ol' days.

MAMA WHEELIS. Well, yew can have 'em. I had to work too hard. But thank the good Lord for F.D.R. and the W.P.A.

EVALITA. God, I hated them summers. I was always the littlest and ya'll never would let me play with yew. Then Mama Wheelis would make me clean house with 'er. Wash dishes, dust, sweep all them hardwood floors. Yud thank I was a slave.

MAMA WHEELIS. I was trainin' yew to be a good housewife. Lord knows where I went wrong.

LURLENE. Evalita, we all had to do chores, too.

SARA LEE. Yew know why we didn't let yew play with us, Evalita?

EVALITA. 'Cause I was the littlest.

SARA LEE. That's a bunch a bosh. That ain't the reason.

ORVILLE. It was 'cause yew was a pain in the ass, Evalita.

MAMA WHEELIS. Watch yure mouth.

ORVILLE. They even say ass in the Bible, Mama Wheelis.

MAMA WHEELIS. Well, yew ain't in the Bible. Yure in Lowake.

SARA LEE. *(Getting angry for no apparent reason.)* Orville's right. Yew was a pain in the ass, Evalita. Yew whined when yew wouldn't git your way. You wouldn't play fair...always cheated at ever' game we played. Threw rocks at us. Yew was mean. A mean spoiled little brat. Daddy spoiled yew rotten.

LURLENE. *(This is out of line.)* Sara Lee...

EVALITA. What are yew gittin' so fired up about? That was when we was all kids.

SARA LEE. Was, Evalita. But we ain't kids enymore. Dudn't ever'body agree with me that it's high time Miss Evalita grow up?

LURLENE. Sara Lee...please.

EVALITA. What are yew talkin' about, girl?

SARA LEE. Yew know damn well what I'm talkin' about, "girl."

ORVILLE. Maybe we ought to find that strong box and git Daddy's affairs in order.

SARA LEE. Shut up, Orville.

LURLENE. Should one of us be lookin' in on Daddy? Maybe we could all go together and check...

SARA LEE. Shut up, Lurlene.

LURLENE. *(upset)* Well, boy, oh boy! *(SARA LEE turns to MAMA WHEELIS expecting her to say something.)*

MAMA WHEELIS. I ain't sayin' a word.

SARA LEE. I've tried to ignore this, but I jest cain't enymore. *(Takes a deep breath.)* What did yew and Clarence do last night, Evalita.

EVALITA. Oh, now I git it.

ORVILLE. Well, I don't. Would someone fill me in?

SARA LEE. Shut up, Orville! I'm waitin', Evalita.

EVALITA. Sara Lee. I am still young. Sometimes my youth gits in the ways of my mind.

SARA LEE. Don't flatter yureself, Evalita. Yew ain't that young. In fact, yew are old...real old. Older than enyone in this room. Even older than Mama Wheelis.

EVALITA. What the hell yew talkin' about?

MAMA WHEELIS. *(To LURLENE.)* Did she say that Evalita's older than me?

ORVILLE. She talkin' nonsense.

EVALITA. *(Starts to walk out.)* I don't have to listen to this.

SARA LEE. No, Orville, I ain't talkin' nonsense. Otherwise yew'd understand me, since that's the only language yew know.

ORVILLE. Now yew jest wait a dad burn minute.

SARA LEE. Shut up! *(Runs in front of Evalita, blocking the door.)* And Evalita, don't yew dare walk out that door 'cause I'll be on yew like stink on shit. *(EVALITA tries to get past her; SARA LEE holds her.)*

MAMA WHEELIS. I wish I had me a roast in the oven to check on...but I don't. *(She continues to snap beans and watches.)*

SARA LEE. Yeah, Missy, yew are old. Older than me,

older than Lurlene...older than Mama Wheelis. But yew don't act like it. Yew jest look like it. See, Evalita...people who live like yew git old real fast. Yew put a hunderd thousand miles on a brand new car and the car may still be new...but the engine is worn out. Parts wear out...if yew catch my drift, Evalita. *(EVALITA continues to try to get past Sara Lee, but it is no use.)*

MAMA WHEELIS. *(To Lurlene.)* I ain't quite shore what she's gittin' at.

LURLENE. *(whispering)* I'll explain later.

SARA LEE. *(continuing)* Yew been rode hard, Evalita. Real hard. And many many times. And it's fin'ly catchin' up ta yew. Even yure face looks old. *(Grabbing her face, EVALITA slaps at SARA LEE'S hand.)* Chisel off all that make-up and we'd have a Texas road map.

LURLENE. That's enough, Sara Lee.

SARA LEE. Yew ain't Mama, Lurlene.

EVALITA. *(Rushes SARA LEE trying to get out, SARA LEE pushes her, continuing to block the door; breaking down.)* I do not have ta listen to this shit.

LURLENE. Please...ya'll stop.

SARA LEE. *(Grabs EVALITA'S arm and pushes her back.)* Yes yew do 'cause I ain't done. The only thang yew have goin' fer yew, honey, is that yure willin'. Willin' ta do it with enyone in pants. Willin' ta bed flop with enythang that moves. God, I hate yew fer that. We all do. I hate that my baby sister is nothin' but a slut...a little two-bit whore. *(LURLENE and MAMA WHEELIS gasp.)*

LURLENE. Sara Lee, stop it!

MAMA WHEELIS. I thank that's enough, Sara Lee.

ORVILLE. More than enough.

EVALITA. *(Crying; rushing SARA LEE; SARA LEE slaps her back.)* Yew are viscious, Sara Lee. *(An all-out fight is about to happen.)*

LURLENE. *(Throwing herself between them.)* Please, stop! *(In one move, SARA LEE pushes her out of the way.)*

SARA LEE. But I'm honest.

EVALITA. *(Attacking SARA LEE.)* Like hell yew are.

LURLENE. *(Getting physical, pulling them apart.)* I mean it. Right now...

SARA LEE. *(Turning on LURLENE; really throwing her across the room out of the way.)* Don't tell me what to do, Lurlene. Yew don't have the right. *(To EVALITA.)* I have one question to ask yew and I want a straight answer. *(pause)* Did yew sleep with Clarence last night?

LURLENE. Oh, please.

SARA LEE. Shut up, Lurlene.

MAMA WHEELIS. Good lord.

ORVILLE. This is gittin' good. Come on, Evalita, answer her.

EVERYONE. Shut up, Orville!

SARA LEE. Yes or no? Did yew sleep with my fiance Clarence Hopkins last night?

EVALITA. *(Regaining her composure.)* Well, yew know Clarence and yew know me...so I thank yew have the answer to yure question. Now if yew'll excuse me, I'm goin' to go down to Bluebell's and git drunk. And maybe I'll even git lucky agin. *(SARA LEE is stung as EVALITA starts to exit out the front door; turning back.)* Yew may have the wool pulled over ever'body else's eyes Sara Lee...but I been out around this town...and I know the truth. *(She storms out.)*

SARA LEE. *(Goes after her letting out a loud scream.)* Why yew little bitch! *(EVALITA starts running away, SARA LEE after her, LURLENE after SARA LEE; O.S.)* Yew better run or I'll kick yure ass all the way to Odessa. *(LURLENE drags SARA LEE back on stage, SARA LEE resisting.)*

LURLENE. *(Holding onto SARA LEE's arm.)* Just calm down, Sara Lee.

SARA LEE. Leave me alone. *(breaking loose)* And let go a my arm.

LURLENE. I was just tryin' to help.

SARA LEE. Well, yew ain't helpin'. And who the hell do yew thank yew are, Lurlene? Huh? Yew thank yew can jest waltz in here ever' five or ten years, take over and boss ever'body around? Huh?

LURLENE. Well, no, I...

SARA LEE. *(continuing)* Yew ain't Mama, Lurlene. And don't yew ever try ta be. Yew know, I was here, Lurlene. I was here all along. Here when yew and J.D. up and left...here when Orville decided to git off his fat ass and move ta Snyder...and here when Evalita hit the road and sought out husband after husband.

LURLENE. Sara Lee, you certainly didn't have to...

SARA LEE. *(interrupting)* Oh, yeah? Then who was gonna take care of Daddy and Mama Wheelis?

MAMA WHEELIS. I can take care of myself, thank you very much.

SARA LEE. Then what about Daddy? No offense, Mama Wheelis, but yew are gettin' on up there.

MAMA WHEELIS. Thanks fer remindin' me. Us old folks tend to ferget.

SARA LEE. I had to. I had to stay. Right here in Podunk

Lowake. Dumb ol' Sara Lee. Rattin' hair, takin' care of
Mama Wheelis and Daddy and gittin' old.

MAMA WHEELIS. Well, join the crowd.

SARA LEE. *(continuing)* Well, I'm tired of it. I'm tired of
ever'body takin' me fer granted. I'm gonna lose Daddy.
And now I've lost Clarence too. I jest ain't no good with
men. *(silence)* I'd like ta make a phone call. Could ya'll
leave me alone, please.

LURLENE. I'll go check on Daddy. *(She Exits.)*

MAMA WHEELIS. Orville, there's somethin' in the cellar
that I need yew ta hep me with.

ORVILLE. Is it heavy?

MAMA WHEELIS. Git up off yure bohunkus and help me
right this minute before I git my razor strap after yew.
Wait fer me on the back porch.

ORVILLE. *(Reluctantly Exiting out through the kitchen.)*
Okay, but I've been down in my back lately and we're
lible to git heat stroke.

MAMA WHEELIS. Git!!

LURLENE. *(returns)* For what it's worth, Sara Lee. I am
sorry. *(She Exits.)*

SARA LEE. What a little bitch.

MAMA WHEELIS. Watch yure mouth. *(pause)* Who?

SARA LEE. Evalita.

MAMA WHEELIS. Sara Lee, lyin' ain't no good. I don't
know why yew told 'em that.

SARA LEE. Don't lecture me, Mama Wheelis.

MAMA WHEELIS. I shoulda never lied fer ya, baby.

SARA LEE. *(starting to cry)* I jest didn't want 'em ta
know.

MAMA WHEELIS. *(Hugs her.)* I know.

ORVILLE. *(O.S.)* Are yew comin', Mama Wheelis? I'm burnin' up.

MAMA WHEELIS. I'm comin', Orville. *(Hugs SARA LEE tighter.)* It'll all turn out, baby. *(She starts to Exit, then turns back.)* Honey, someday I'd like yew ta explain ta me the part about the new car engine and Evalita bein' older than me.

SARA LEE. *(smiles)* Okay. *(MAMA WHEELIS Exits through the kitchen; SARA LEE sits on the couch and thinks for a minute, then goes to the phone. She starts to dial, then decides not to. She lights a cigarette, paces some, then goes to the telephone, stares at it, then picks it up and dials so fast that she can't change her mind.)* Hello, Otis. Can I speak ta Clarence, please? *(pause)* Clarence...it's me, Sara Lee. *(She starts to break, barely able to talk, takes a moment to recover.)* How could yew, Clarence? How could yew do this ta me? *(pause)* Nevermind. Yew don't owe me a explanation. *(Trying very hard not to lose it.)* Clarence, I need a big favor...for ol' times sake, okay? *(pause)* I need, well, I need...I told my whole family we was gittin' married. I even bought a fake engagement ring. *(Laughing on the verge of tears.)* They bought it too...hook, line and sinker. Idn't that funny? So, now that this has happened with yew and Evalita... *(pause)* Please don't play dumb with me, Clarence. I jest don't want ta eat crow...especially served by her. *(pause)* Okay, okay. Jest tell 'er we're gittin' married, okay? *(pause)* And, Clarence, I know I'm askin' an awful lot...but please don't sleep with her agin. Tell 'er she's too old or that she wadn't no good or somethin'. *(pause)* Well, Clarence, that's two diff'rent stories...one from yew and one from

Jezebel...and I shore as hell wouldn't take eny bets on who's lyin' and who's tellin' the truth. *(Pause, then she hangs up; softly.)* And I still love yew too, Clarence. *(She puts out her cigarette, buries her head in her hands, and breaks down.)*

(BUFORD Enters from the hallway entrance, wearing a robe and pajamas, walking very slowly towards SARA LEE. She doesn't see him until he sits down beside her. She looks at him, then puts her head on his shoulder. He hugs her.)

SARA LEE. Oh, Daddy.

BUFORD. It's alright, punkin.

SARA LEE. Daddy, I don't want yew ta die. Yew're the only man who ever really loved me.

BUFORD. *(Talking to her like she's six years old.)* Shh...it'll be alright. Daddy's here. Daddy'll take care of his sweet punkin. Hush up. It'll be jest fine. Shh. Yew want Daddy to sang to ya? Huh? Is that what my sweet little punkin wants?

SARA LEE. Yes, Daddy.

BUFORD. *(Singing very softly as if to a baby.)* "Hush little baby, don't say a word. Daddy's gonna buy yew a mockin' bird, And if that mockin' bird won't sang, Daddy's gonna buy yew a diamond ring. And if that diamond ring turns brass, Daddy's..."

(LURLENE rushes into the living room.)

LURLENE. Daddy's gone. I went to the bathroom...

BUFORD. Shh, Linnie Sue. I'm puttin' the baby ta

sleep. *(LURLENE stands and watches, SARA LEE with her head on his shoulder, her eyes closed; he continues his song.)* "And if that diamond ring turns brass, Daddy's gonna buy yew a lookin' glass.

(The LIGHTS begin to dim.)

BUFORD. And if that lookin' glass turns brown, Yew'll still be the sweetest little girl in town."

(The LIGHTS grow dimmer, until:)

BLACKOUT

Scene 2

*AT RISE: One hour later...MARLENE and HARMONY walk in
the front door. They have been smoking marijuana.
MARLENE is giggling as she talks. The PHONE is
ringing.*

MARLENE. So me and my sister Vanitta made these
dresses. Hers was pink and mine was lime green. *(Answers
phone.)* Hello, Turnover-Wheelis residence.

HARMONY. *(laughing)* Why don't you just say,
"hello?"

MARLENE. *(Covers receiver.)* Shut up, Harmony. *(She continues to giggle.)*

HARMONY. Damn, that was good shit.

MARLENE. *(giggling)* This is Marlene Turnover.

HARMONY. I've got the munchies.

MARLENE. *(To HARMONY.)* Me too. *(to phone)* Why,
hello, Maybelline. *(HARMONY finds his rice cakes and starts
eating them. He offers one to Marlene and she eats as she talks.)*
Fine, jest fine. Are yew still fat, Maybelline? *(HARMONY
starts laughing, so does MARLENE, she tries to shush him.)* Shh.
Well, I've lost weight.

HARMONY. *(Mimicking EVALITA.)* Well, look behind
yew and yew'll find it.

MARLENE. *(laughing)* I'm sorry, but someone's makin'
me laugh. *(pause)* Uh, it's Orville. *(Continuing to laugh.)*
Yew know what a cut-up he is. *(Covering the receiver.)* Shut

82

up, Orville. *(Laughs even harder; she hangs up on Maybelline. The PHONE rings again. HARMONY grabs it.)*

HARMONY. *(Holding his nose and mimicking a female operator.)* The number you have reached is out of order. Please check the number and try your call again. This is a recording. *(He hangs up and they are doubled over in laughter when the PHONE rings again; HARMONY picks it up.)* Dammit, I said it was out of order! *(He hangs up and they are now hysterical.)*

MARLENE. Damn I'm hungry and these rice thangies ain't gonna cut it. *(She Exits to the kitchen and continues the dialogue as she brings out everything from the refrigerator and sets up on the coffee table.)*

HARMONY. So tell me about your lime green dress.

MARLENE. Oh yeah...me and my sister Vanitta made these dresses. Hers was pink and mine was lime green. They was the exact same pattern. *(Starts to laugh again.)* Gawd they was ugly. Had these big ol' bows right across the front of our boobs. *(She and HARMONY commence to pig out on their spread.)* So, we went to the prom...stag. Now Vanitta was bigger than me and I was weighing in well over 200 then. Boy, we was a sight for sore eyes. We was one whole row of wallflowers. *(They start to laugh again as they eat.)* Orville was datin' ugly ol' Wilma Burns then, had big ol' buck teeth and long stringy hair and no eyebrows. He wouldn't even give me the time a day, even though he was big as a barn, too. Don't ask me why, but I had the biggest crush on him then. Damn this pie is good. So, the band started playin' Chubby Checker's "The Twist," and yew shoulda seen Orville. Yew want a sandwich of leftover pot roast?

HARMONY. I'm a vegetarian, but what the hell.

MARLENE. So Orville started twistin' and shoutin' and shoutin' and twistin'. *(She starts to laugh, not able to continue.)*

HARMONY. *(laughing)* Go on...what happened?

MARLENE. *(Laughing through the line.)* And he twisted so hard that he split his pants. He was so caught up in the twist that he didn't even notice. *(She hands HARMONY the sandwich and keeps talking, eating and laughing like there's no tomorrow.)*

HARMONY. Thanks.

MARLENE. *(continuing)* Well, Vanitta saw it first and pointed to Orville and I 'bout hit the floor. His big ol' butt hangin' out of his suit pants. Damn this pot roast is good. And he had a big ol' hole in his underwear. I laughed so hard I wet my pants. *(They are laughing hysterical again.)*

HARMONY. You didn't.

MARLENE. I sure as hell did. Had to leave the prom ...didn't even dance once. Vanitta was so mad at me. She was drivin'. Oh God, it was a sight. Big ol' hole in his underwear...yew could even see his crack.

HARMONY. *(So intrigued with this lady.)* Marlene, you are a funny woman.

MARLENE. I ain't never smoked marijuana cigarettes before. It was a first fer me.

HARMONY. And a pretty woman.

MARLENE. They make me talk too much, though.

HARMONY. They make me horny.

MARLENE. Oh, my stars. *(HARMONY touches her arm gently.)* Stop it. Please. Harmony! *(He kisses her neck.)* Don't do that, Harmony, please. *(He continues.)* Funny and pretty, huh?

HARMONY. And neat. *(He stares into her eyes and continues to romance her.)*

MARLENE. Ooh. Oh my goodness. Stop. *(She doesn't want to give in, but...; he continues.)* And neat, huh?

HARMONY. And fun. I can't remember when I've had so much fun. *(He continues to kiss her on the neck and down her arm.)*

MARLENE. Oh, stop. I'm gittin'...

HARMONY. Horny?

MARLENE. Yeah. No! Confused. Nobody's ever told me those thangs. *(He kisses her full on the lips. She indulges for a moment, then breaks away.)* Oh, stop it, Harmony. Someone's gonna catch us. We cain't do this. Now stop. *(She suddenly grabs him and they kiss for a long time.)*

HARMONY. I think I'm falling in love with you, Marlene.

MARLENE. *(She breaks away again.)* Yew cain't. That's impossible. Yew jest cain't. I don't know what I'm doin'. It's them marijuana cigarettes. Yew jest cain't. I got a fat mean husband and a kid in reform school.

HARMONY. *(He softly kisses her face.)* I know.

MARLENE. Ooh. Aw. Now stop it. *(weakly)* I mean it... *(They are passionate again.)*

HARMONY. Run away with me, Marlene.

MARLENE. I cain't. Stop it, Harmony. Please.

HARMONY. I can't.

MARLENE. It ain't right.

HARMONY. It ain't right?

MARLENE. It ain't moral. Jest stop it, please.

HARMONY. Somehow, I don't think it's very right...or moral for you to be miserable with that lousy son-of-a-bitch who treats you like shit.

MARLENE. We had some good years.

HARMONY. You're unhappy, Marlene.

MARLENE. What are yew talkin' about? I'm happy.

HARMONY. With me...for the last two hours. You've only been happy once since you got here. And that was with me.

MARLENE. *(Starts to cry.)* Stop it. Stop sayin' those thangs.

HARMONY. Why? *(No answer.)* 'Cause they're true, Marlene?

MARLENE. No, they ain't true. What about Evalita?

HARMONY. What about her, Marlene? She doesn't love me. She doesn't know what love is. I need a real woman. A sincere woman. An honest woman. A woman who is capable of giving and being loved. I've never felt like this in my whole life, Marlene. I want to spend the rest of my life with you.

MARLENE. Oh, Harmony. The way yew talk. *(They kiss a long passionate kiss.)*

ORVILLE. *(O.S. headed for the living room; calling out.)* Marlene, git your butt movin' and help me find that damn key...and brang me a beer, pronto!

MARLENE. *(Pushes HARMONY away and dives into the pie, grabbing a whole piece, cramming it into her mouth; HARMONY also grabs a piece.)* This is the best pie. I wish I could bake like Mama Wheelis.

(ORVILLE Enters from hallway.)

ORVILLE. Well, well, well...what have we here? A hipp-y and a hipp-o.

MARLENE. We was hungry. So we fixed a little snack.

ORVILLE. Little, my ass.

(MAMA WHEELIS comes through the hallway into the living room.)

MAMA WHEELIS. Orville, what was yew doin' in the back bedroom? It looks like a tornada hit it. *(Seeing MARLENE'S "snack.")* Well, help me, hanner. What is this?

MARLENE. We was hungry.

MAMA WHEELIS. Well, git that off my coffee table right this minute. I jest Pledged it this mornin'.

ORVILLE. What happened to "Git lean with Herbalean," Marlene?

HARMONY. *(To MAMA WHEELIS.)* Good pie.

MAMA WHEELIS. Thank you, Hominy. Marlene, move that stuff, right now. Eat it on the table. *(MARLENE starts to clear the coffee table.)*

ORVILLE. "Bye, Bye, Herbalean. Bye, bye, Marlene. Hello, fatso. I thank I'm gonna die."

MARLENE. I can have one meal a day.

ORVILLE. One meal, my ass.

MAMA WHEELIS. Watch it.

ORVILLE. Well, that's enough food to feed a army.

MARLENE. *(On the verge of tears.)* Well, Harmony was eatin' too.

HARMONY. Good pie.

MAMA WHEELIS. Orville, what was yew doin' in

Buford's room, goin' through all his thangs?

ORVILLE. I was tryin' to find the key to Daddy's strong box.

MARLENE. Yew're mean, Orville.

ORVILLE. I ain't mean.

MARLENE. Puttin' my only boy in reform school, makin' fun a me...yew are too mean.

ORVILLE. *(Grabs her arm.)* I ain't mean. I'm jest seein' what's going on, that's all. And leave Jimbo outta this. I knew this wouldn't last. Yew're gonna blow up bigger than Lulu on Hee Haw. Once yew start, yew cain't stop, and yew know it.

MARLENE. *(Suddenly pulling away from him.)* Shut up! Jest leave me alone!

ORVILLE. I can hear it now. All them hens down at the beauty shop. "Oh, honey, look at Marlene. Lost all that weight. Now she's bigger'n Dallas." *(laughs)* I cain't wait.

MARLENE. *(mad, starts crying)* Jest shut up, Orville. Yew never have one kind word to say to me. Not one kind word. But yure gonna be sorry some day. and then it'll be too late. *(She starts for the front door.)*

ORVILLE. Where the hell yew thank yure goin'?

MARLENE. Out! *(She slams the door in his face.)*

MAMA WHEELIS. That *was* mean, Orville. Real mean.

ORVILLE. *(exploding)* Don't tell me how ta talk to my own damn wife. I'm a grown man, Mama Wheelis. *(MAMA WHEELIS starts gathering up the rest of the food on the coffee table very upset. As he passes HARMONY.)* And yew, hippy boy. Yew stay outta my way.

HARMONY. No, problem. *(ORVILLE Exits through the*

kitchen.) Lard ass.

MAMA WHEELIS. *(almost defeated)* Watch yure mouth.

(SARA LEE walks out from the hallway in a bathrobe, wearing a shower cap.)

SARA LEE. What was all that comotion?

MAMA WHEELIS. It was jest Orville and Marlene.

SARA LEE. *(Comforting MAMA WHEELIS who is visibly upset.)* Oh. I heard the phone ring, Mama Wheelis. Was it for me?

MAMA WHEELIS. I don't thank so, honey. But me and Lurlene was takin' a nap. Lurlene's still asleep.

SARA LEE. Well, I don't see how.

HARMONY. Marlene answered it. I cain't remember her name. It was someone fat.

SARA LEE and MAMA WHEELIS. Maybelline.

SARA LEE. Harmony, yure eyes look funny. Are yew feelin' alright?

HARMONY. I'm fine. Just stressed.

MAMA WHEELIS. I hear ya there, boy.

(ORVILLE Enters from kitchen with a crowbar.)

ORVILLE. I found a crowbar. I'll have this baby opened in no time.

SARA LEE. Where'd yew find the strong box?

ORVILLE. It was in the cellar. Mama Wheelis showed it to me. But we cain't find the key.

MAMA WHEELIS. It had slipped my mind, but I seen Buford take it down there a coupla weeks ago. We cain't find the key, though.

ORVILLE. No problem. I'll have this opened in no time. *(HARMONY continues to stare at ORVILLE. O.S. MARLENE and EVALITA are singing a Christmas carol.)*

MAMA WHEELIS. *(Going to the window.)* What in the world?

ORVILLE. *(disgusted)* What now? *(He's sweating with every effort to open the box.)*

SARA LEE. Who is that, Mama Wheelis?

HARMONY. Sounds like Christmas carolers.

ORVILLE. It ain't Christmas!!

HARMONY. Oh.

MAMA WHEELIS. It's Evalita and Marlene. They're drunk as a coupla niggers. *(HARMONY flinches.)*

SARA LEE. Mama Wheelis, how many times have I told yew not to say that word? It's offensive.

ORVILLE. Ain't nothin' wrong with callin' a spade a spade.

HARMONY. *(Lets out a loud scream of frustration; everyone stares at him.)* I'm sorry, I just had to do that.

(LURLENE comes running in from the hallway.)

LURLENE. What's wrong? I heard a scream.

(EVALITA and MARLENE storm in the house singing a Christmas carol; EVALITA holding a beer in one hand and the rest of the carton in the other.)

EVALITA. *(announcing)* We're drunk.

SARA LEE. No shit.

MAMA WHEELIS. Watch it.

MARLENE. I ain't drunk. I'm high on marijuana cigarettes...

MAMA WHEELIS. Good lord!

LURLENE. You're lucky you didn't get arrested.

MARLENE. But I'll git drunk, too. Give me them beers, Evalita. *(She takes the carton.)*

MAMA WHEELIS. Well, now ain't this perty.

ORVILLE. No wonder our boy's in reform school. I oughta...

MARLENE. Yew put 'im there. That's why he's there. But I tell ya what yew *oughta* do. *(She grabs the crowbar from ORVILLE.)* Yew oughta cram this where the sun don't shine.

LURLENE. Oh dear.

MARLENE. *(continuing)* I'm tired of yew, Orville. Real tired. So, yew better watch it. *(She waves the crowbar at him.)*

ORVILLE. There ain't no reasoning with a dope addict. Give me that. *(He tries to grab the crowbar.)*

MARLENE. I'll give it to ya. *(She takes a couple of swings at him. He has to move quickly, barely escaping a blow to his head.)*

SARA LEE. Oh, my goodness.

MAMA WHEELIS. *(overlapping)* Heavens to Betsy.

LURLENE. *(overlapping)* Stop it...now!

MARLENE. *(Gives him the crowbar.)* Here. I jest wanted to see how fast a asshole could move. Yew bore the shit outta me.

MAMA WHEELIS. I am washing my hands of this whole fam'ly.

MARLENE. *(Gives Orville a look.)* I'm gonna git drunk...now.

ORVILLE. Yew don't need them beers.

MARLENE. Yew better shut up! *(Walks over to HAR-MONY.)* Harmony, my good friend, yew wanna beer?

HARMONY. *(taking one)* What the hell. *(ORVILLE continues to try and get the strong box open.)*

EVALITA. *(very drunk)* Is Daddy's will in that box?

ORVILLE. Yeah. Sit down and I'll have it opened in no time.

MAMA WHEELIS. Orville, yew sed that ten minutes ago.

ORVILLE. I've almost got it. *(Harmony lets out a big belch.)*

MARLENE. *(Laughing, taking the blame.)* 'Cuse me. I didn't mean to do that.

EVALITA. Well now, ain't this exciting. Sittin' around listenin' to people burp and watchin' a fool tryin' to open a box. I giss we'll all be goin' downtown to watch lightin' bugs fly around the street lamp for this evenin's entertainment.

MAMA WHEELIS. Naw, Evalita. I'm shore yew could sniff out another honkey-tonk in no time if yew set yure mind to it.

HARMONY. I can open that box.

ORVILLE. What?

HARMONY. I said, I can open that box.

MAMA WHEELIS. He's sayin' he can open Buford's strong box.

ORVILLE. How?

SARA LEE. Come on, Orville. Let 'im open it.

EVALITA. I hope that will's in there.

ORVILLE. I'll have it opened in a second with this crowbar.

MARLENE. *(Grabs the crowbar again; ORVILLE ducks; she hands it to HARMONY.)* Open it, Harmony.

HARMONY. I don't need this. *(He puts the crowbar down.)* I need a hairpin. *(MARLENE, LURLENE, MAMA WHEELIS, SARA LEE, and EVALITA all offer a hairpin to HARMONY. He looks at EVALITA, then takes the one from MARLENE. They exchange smiles. HARMONY starts picking the lock.)*

EVALITA. Harmony's real handy around the house, if yew know what I mean.

MAMA WHEELIS. We don't wanna know what yew mean, Evalita.

SARA LEE. I thought ya'll lived in that hippy wagon out front like white trash.

LURLENE. Sara Lee...

EVALITA. Only when we tour.

SARA LEE. *(Giving LURLENE and MAMA WHEELIS a look.)* When they "tour."

ORVILLE. Havin' a little trouble there, Harmony?

HARMONY. *(Popping the lock open.)* Not at all.

MAMA WHEELIS. My lord, that hippy's a crook.

HARMONY. Was, Mama Wheelis. I did some time for armed robbery, but it was a bum rap.

LURLENE. My goodness.

MAMA WHEELIS. *(Whispering as she takes LURLENE'S arm and ushers her towards the hallway.)* Lurlene, come hep me hide my jew'ry. *(They Exit.)*

EVALITA. I didn't know yew had been in the pen.

HARMONY. Does it matter to you?

ORVILLE. *(Getting a little nervous.)* What the hell...let's let bygones be bygones.

EVALITA. Yes, Harmony, it does matter to me.

ORVILLE. Hell, Evalita...that third husband a yures ...Dave, Darrell...Dale...whatever-the-hell-his-name-was went to the pen in Huntsville for writin' hot checks. What the hell do yew care?

EVALITA. I divorced him, didn't I? Maybe Mama Wheelis was right. Maybe I do pick losers.

HARMONY. *(Starting for the front door.)* Excuse me.

EVALITA. Harmony, wait. I'm sorry. I didn't mean that. *(She grabs his arm.)* I'm not myself. I've been drankin'...(*He slams the door in her face. MARLENE runs to the window and watches him.)* Shit. I shouldn't sed that. He's been good ta me.

MARLENE. And yew treated him like dirt.

(MAMA WHEELIS Enters with LURLENE, looking around for HARMONY.)

SARA LEE. He's gone, Mama Wheelis.

MAMA WHEELIS. That give me a scere. I like that boy, but I have that diamond broach that Buster Daddy give me that's worth a fortune. I hated Buster, but I shore love that broach.

MARLENE. He wouldn'ta stole the broach. *(She Exits down the hallway.)*

ORVILLE. Well, let's git this show on the road. *(They all gather around; ORVILLE opens the box.)* Here we are.

LURLENE. *(spotting something)* Oh looky here...(*She picks up some bronzed baby shoes.)* It's my baby shoes... bronzed.

SARA LEE. *(Picks up a piece of paper.)* And here's one of my report cards. Straight A's. I shoulda gone to college like yew, Lurlene.

LURLENE. Oh, you did very well for yourself and you know it.

MAMA WHEELIS. Yure the best beauty operator in Lowake.

SARA LEE. I'm the only beauty operator in Lowake.

EVALITA. Where's the will?

ORVILLE. *(Picks up a rock.)* Would yew look at this. It's an arrowhead. I found it and gave it to Daddy when I was five years old on Father's Day.

SARA LEE. Daddy's real sentimental, idn't he?

MAMA WHEELIS. There's the newspaper clippin' about Linnie Sue when she died. *(Takes it and looks at it; there is a moment of silence.)*

EVALITA. Could we jest take a short cut down mem'ry lane and find the goddamn will?

MAMA WHEELIS. I was jest about to tear up, Evalita. Thank yew fer ruinin' my moment.

ORVILLE. I don't see it, but I'm sure it's here 'cause Daddy kept ever' thang important in this strong box. *(He continues to look.)*

EVALITA. Yeah, that arrowhead ranks right up there.

SARA LEE. He ain't dead, yet.

LURLENE. What?

SARA LEE. I sed...he ain't dead yet.

MAMA WHEELIS. She's sayin' that Buford ain't dead, yet.

ORVILLE. *(keeps looking)* Nobody sed he was, Sara Lee.

SARA LEE. Yew said, "Daddy kept." It shoulda been Daddy keeps ever'thang in that strong box 'cause he...*(Chokes up.)*...ain't dead yet.

MAMA WHEELIS. We know he ain't dead, honey. He's asleep in the back bedroom.

(MARLENE returns through the hallway entrance.)

MARLENE. Well, are yew all millionaires, yet?

EVALITA. *(Who has been digging in the box.)* I found it! *(She opens it.)* Yeah, this is it! *(reading)* "Last Will and Testament"...oh my lord. Ya'll ain't gonna believe this. Damn, I was right. It sez here his estate has been appraised at six hunderd thousand dollars!

MARLENE. *(Looks around the room.)* Well, it ain't in real estate.

ORVILLE. Let me see that. *(He grabs the will.)*

EVALITA. *(Grabs it back.)* I ain't done.

SARA LEE. Why don't yew read it out loud, Evalita?

LURLENE. That's a good idea.

EVALITA. *(Her expression changes.)* Oh, my God.

ORVILLE. What is it?

SARA LEE. What's wrong?

EVALITA. I cain't read it out loud. Here, Sara Lee...yew read it.

LURLENE. Well, what is it?

ORVILLE. Read it, Sara Lee.

SARA LEE. *(reading)* "I Buford Wyman Turnover, being of sound mind and body do hereby..."

ORVILLE. Git to the good part.

SARA LEE. *(Searches for it, then reads again.)* "My home

shall be left to Sara Lee Turnover and Lois Wheelis until the death of Lois Wheelis whereby it shall be the property of Sara Lee Turnover."

MAMA WHEELIS. Whew...at least I ain't out on the streets.

SARA LEE. *(continuing)* "The rest of my estate shall be divided equally among Sara Lee Turnover, Evalita Latrelle Turnover Wilson...

EVALITA. That was when I was married to Darrell.

SARA LEE. *(Looking up at LURLENE; pause; hesitantly.)* Lurlene, he sed he made a mistake.

LURLENE. I'm not in it, am I? *(SARA LEE shakes her head.)*

ORVILLE. What about me? *(SARA LEE hands the will to ORVILLE; searches.)* Let's see. *(reacting)* I knew it. I *have* done peed in my chili.

LURLENE. It's alright. I never expected anything anyway.

ORVILLE. Well, I did.

MARLENE. *(Grabs the will from ORVILLE.)* Well, there goes that motor boat yew wanted. *(Started to laugh as she reads it.)*

MAMA WHEELIS. What's so funny, Marlene?

MARLENE. He scratched Orville's name out and wrote in the Lowake Pool and Dominoe Hall.

MAMA WHEELIS. That pool hall's about to go under.

MARLENE. Not enymore. *(She laughs some more.)*

SARA LEE. That may not hold up legally, Orville ...'cause it was handwritten.

MARLENE. Yeah, it will. It's initialed and witnessed by Liddy Bell Cartwright and Clara Bell Ivey and notarized...by Mama Wheelis. That makes it legal. *(LURLENE takes the will and starts to read it.)*

SARA LEE. You notarized his will, Mama Wheelis? Why didn't you tell us?

MAMA WHEELIS. *(Struggling for a good excuse.)* It had slipped my mind. *(softly)* You know how us old people tend to fergit.

LURLENE. I can't believe ya'll missed this. He didn't leave me out. Right here in number five it says. "I leave my daughter Lurlene Sue Rogers one dollar." Anybody need a loan? *(Nobody laughs.)*

MARLENE. *(To ORVILLE.)* That means yew'll git a dollar too, Orville. Even though it don't say it...'cause I believe it's the law.

ORVILLE. A buck! I cain't believe it. *(He takes the will and looks it over one more time.)* One measly buck.

EVALITA. This is jest awful.

ORVILLE. One measly buck...

EVALITA. *(not meaning it)* I'm jest sick over this.

ORVILLE. One measly buck.

MAMA WHEELIS. I've got an idea. Since Evalita feels so awful about this...why don't Sara Lee and Evalita split their part with Orville and Lurlene?

EVALITA. It ain't that awful.

SARA LEE. I'm willin' to give some of mine away.

EVALITA. Well, I got so many expenses with my record and all...I jest don't thank I can afford it. I've been countin' on this.

MAMA WHEELIS. Buford ought'na left yew a dime. I tried my best to talk him out of it.

EVALITA. Jest shut up, Mama Wheelis!

LURLENE. *(wheeling)* Don't you ever tell her to shut up again or you'll be sprawled out on that floor not knowing what hit you. I've had enough of you and I'm tired of being nice. Yew know, Evalita, I really don't care about that money, but let me remind you of a time when you and Timmy Lee Smith...that boy you called your first husband, were broke and J.D. and I paid your rent and bought you a month's supply of groceries.

EVALITA. That was a long time ago, Lurlene. I did say thank you, didn't I?

LURLENE. Nevermind. You're hopeless.

EVALITA. Hopeless?

LURLENE. Yeah, hopeless, Evalita. With a capital H.

EVALITA. Well, at least I didn't try to mercy kill Daddy.

LURLENE. What?

SARA LEE. Shut up, Evalita.

MAMA WHEELIS. *(overlapping)* Good Lord.

LURLENE. No, wait a minute. I want to hear this one. Go on, Evalita.

EVALITA. Well, Dr. Wetzel sed there was some strong medication in Daddy's blood...

LURLENE. I know what Dr. Wetzel said. So, you think I was trying to kill Daddy?

EVALITA. I wouldn't put it past yew. Orville and Sara Lee thought so, too. Sounded like one of yure Christian missions ta me.

LURLENE. Is that true, Sara Lee...Orville? Did ya'll think I tried to kill Daddy?

ORVILLE. Well, I, uh, just thought...

MARLENE. I never thought that, Lurlene.

LURLENE. Thank you, Marlene. Sara Lee?

SARA LEE. When Dr. Wetzel sed that...well, it crossed my mind because yew was the one givin' 'im his medication...but then after'n I thought about it, I knew yew wouldn't do somethin' like that.

EVALITA. Yew didn't speak ta Daddy for ten years, Lurlene. What'd yew expect?

LURLENE. *(Tears filling her eyes.)* Not this.

SARA LEE. *(Puts her arm around LURLENE.)* We didn't mean...

LURLENE. *(Pushing her away.)* Just leave me alone. *(pause)* I guess this is all over town by now. You know what I oughta do? I ought to sue every one of you for slander. Maybe for about two hundred thousand dollars each.

ORVILLE. Yew cain't sue me. I only got a buck.

LURLENE. You know...for all I know, one of you gave him that medication. I knew I wasn't going to be in that will. It seems to me that one of you would have more of a motive to hasten Daddy's death than me.

EVALITA. That's bullshit.

MAMA WHEELIS. I give Buford that medicine.

SARA LEE. What?

MAMA WHEELIS. When I broke my hip, Dr. Wetzel give me these pills fer the pain. They always made me go ta sleep. I jest give 'em to 'im when I thought he needed some rest. I wadn't tryin' ta mercy kill 'im.

SARA LEE. Mama Wheelis, yew shouldn't done that.

MAMA WHEELIS. Well, I did...so what can we do about it now?

(HARMONY walks in the front door.)

SARA LEE. I'm sorry, Lurlene.

ORVILLE. Me too.

EVALITA. *(Spotting HARMONY; not wanting to apologize.)* Well look what the cat drug up. I'm rich, Harmony. My Daddy left me a bundle.

HARMONY. Oh, did he die?

EVALITA. Not yet...but when he does I can cut a whole album and yew can produce it. I am one lucky woman. I'm gonna be rich. And I've got yew and my talent, and now I've got all that money.

HARMONY. Quite frankly,my dear...all you have is the money. I've dumped your things onto the lawn. I'm going back to California. *(MARLENE Exits down the hallway; HARMONY hands EVALITA a tape box.)* Here's your demo tape.

EVALITA. Yew what?

HARMONY. You heard me.

MAMA WHEELIS. Lord, that hippy dumped Evalita.

EVALITA. I'm sorry I called you a loser before, but I was drunk. Now I'm sober...and rich.

(MARLENE enters from hallway, carrying her suitcase.)

MARLENE. I'm going with yew, Harmony.

SARA LEE. Oh, my lord.

ORVILLE. *(Waking up from his daze.)* Yew what?

MARLENE. He asked me to go with 'im and I'm goin'. Yew're right, Harmony. All I have is a fat mean husband and a kid in reform school. I'm goin'.

ORVILLE. *(Getting up and manhandling MARLENE.)* I've had jest about all the lip I'm gonna take from you. Now, yew ain't goin' nowhere, woman, 'cause I'm gonna teach yew a lesson once and for all. *(He starts to hit her; SARA LEE and LURLENE rush to her rescue.)*

SARA LEE. Orville, stop!

LURLENE. *(overlapping)* Orville, no!!

MAMA WHEELIS. *(overlapping)* Not in this house, you don't.

HARMONY. Let go of her, right now.

ORVILLE. The only way you're goin' is over my dead body.

MARLENE. Yew have to sleep sometime.

HARMONY. I said let go of her. Now! *(He pushes ORVILLE away from her, ORVILLE puts up his fists to fight; HARMONY taking a karate stance, leaving ORVILLE very confused.)*

SARA LEE. I wouldn't if I was yew, Orville. They don't play paddycake in the pen.

ORVILLE. *(hesitates; then:)* Aw, who gives a shit enyway. *(Defeated, he goes and sits down on the piano bench.)*

HARMONY. I'm sorry, Evalita...

EVALITA. Aw, shut up!

MAMA WHEELIS. *(Quickly walks over and shakes HARMONY'S hand.)* Nice meetin' yew, Hominy. Keep on sangin'. Yew got a right perty voice. *(chokes up)* And yew take good care of her. *(They hug.)*

HARMONY. I will.

MARLENE. *(Goes to LURLENE and hugs her.)* Bye, Lurlene. Thanks for always bein' nice ta me.

LURLENE. I'll be praying for you, Marlene.

MARLENE. *(Hugs MAMA WHEELIS.)* Bye Mama Wheelis. I love yew.

MAMA WHEELIS. Bye, bye, honey. Be shore ta write. Box 5, Lowake, Texas, 76768.

MARLENE. Bye, Sara Lee. Take good care of yureself. *(Hugs her.)* I hope yew and Clarence git back together.

SARA LEE. Bye, Marlene. I hope yew know what yure doin'.

MARLENE. This time I thank I do. *(She and HARMONY start to leave, she sees ORVILLE and walks over to him; softly.)* Yew took my baby away...and we wadn't never no good together by ourselves.

ORVILLE. Jest leave, Marlene.

MARLENE. I'm takin' Jimbo when he gits out. *(She removes her earrings and wedding ring and hands them to him.)*

EVALITA. *(has had enough)* Jest git outta here...trash!

HARMONY. *(Takes MARLENE'S hand.)* That's us. Let's go. *(She grabs her suitcase; HARMONY takes it from her and they leave out the front door.)*

LURLENE. *(Goes over to ORVILLE.)* Well, the Lord giveth and the Lord taketh away.

BLACKOUT

Scene 3

AT RISE: Mid morning, three days later. As the LIGHTS come up, the PHONE is ringing on an empty stage. MAMA WHELLIS is in the kitchen, talking to someone at the back door.

MAMA WHEELIS. *(O.S.)* Thanks, Clara Bell. I 'preciate it. I'll see ya at the funeral in a little bit. *(Calling out.)* Sara Lee, git that phone, would ya?

SARA LEE. *(O.S.)* I'm in my slip Mama Wheelis.

(MAMA WHEELIS is grumbling as she Enters the living room through the kitchen. She is wearing a black dress, unzipped, a black Sunday-go-to-meetin' hat. She is carrying a bowl and looks under the foil as she sets it on the dining table.)

MAMA WHEELIS. Lord have mercy, lime jello with marshmellas. I'll have to 'frigerate this. Bless 'er heart. She means well. *(The PHONE continues to ring.)*

EVALITA. *(O.S.)* That damn phone is drivin' me crazy.

MAMA WHEELIS. *(Mumbling as she walks to the phone.)* Drivin', huh? *(Answers phone.)*

(There is a KNOCK at the door.)

MAMA WHEELIS. Hello. Well, hello J. D. We're all about ready. *(The KNOCKING continues.)* Hold on, someone's at the door.

(LURLENE Enters; dressed in black.)

LURLENE. I'll get the door.

MAMA WHEELIS. No, yew git the phone. It's yure husband.

LURLENE. Oh.

MAMA WHEELIS. *(Answering the door.)* Hello, Liddy Bell.

LURLENE. *(Picking up the phone.)* Hello, darling.

MAMA WHEELIS. Thanks, honey. I'preciate it. *(She closes the door, walks to the table and looks in the dish.)*

LURLENE. So everything's arranged and all.

MAMA WHEELIS. More lime jello. With pecans.

(SARA LEE Enters in a black dress from hallway entrance.)

SARA LEE. Would somebody zip me?

MAMA WHEELIS. *(Going towards kitchen with both dishes; to SARA LEE.)* Them Ivey girls never could cook. Look at this. Both of 'em brought lime Jello. *(As She Exits to kitchen.)* We'll all be peein' green.

LURLENE. *(Zipping SARA LEE.)* Bye, bye, darlin'.

SARA LEE. *(To LURLENE.)* Thanks.

LURLENE. I'll see you at the church. *(pause)* I love you too. *(She hangs up the phone.)*

SARA LEE. *(To LURLENE.)* Sit down there and I'll touch up yure hair. *(LURLENE sits and SARA LEE works on her hair.)*

LURLENE. That was J.D. He and the boys took care of everything.

SARA LEE. Sometimes it's kinda handy havin' a preacher in the fam'ly.

(MAMA WHEELIS has come out of the kitchen.)

SARA LEE. Come here, Mama Wheelis. Let me zip yure dress.

MAMA WHEELIS. *(Goes over and SARA LEE zips her dress, then she continues with LURLENE's hair.)* I hadn't wore this dress since Finwick's funeral. Pore ol' Finwick.

SARA LEE. Did Clarence call?

MAMA WHEELIS. No, honey.

LURLENE. Mrs. Finwick had the funniest nose.

SARA LEE. I jest thought he might call to say he was sorry about Daddy and all.

MAMA WHEELIS. Well, he didn't call. Honey, that wadn't Finwick's nose.

SARA LEE. He coulda at least called and talked to you, Mama Wheelis. *(She has finished LURLENE'S hair.)* There you go, Lurlene.

LURLENE. Thanks.

MAMA WHEELIS. Honey, he didn't call. He'll prob'ly be at the funeral. He thought the world and all a Buford. *(To LURLENE.)* See, honey, Finwick died eat up with cancer and it started in her nose.

LURLENE. In her nose? *(SARA LEE lights a cigarette and looks out the window.)*

MAMA WHEELIS. Yes, ma'am. So they cut it off. All of it. And they brought in a piece of paper with drawin's of a bunch a noses...all shapes, all sizes and told her they was gonna make 'er a new one and she could take her pick.

LURLENE. Plastic surgery.

MAMA WHEELIS. No, honey, it wadn't plastic. It was real skin. They took it from her hip. *(SARA LEE and LURLENE exchange smiles.)* Finwick coulda took her pick a eny of them noses and she picked that un. For the life a me, I never could understand it.

SARA LEE. We better hurry if we're gonna practice that song.

MAMA WHEELIS. *(Calling out.)* Orville, Evalita...ya'll hurry up. We gotta practice "In the Garden."

LURLENE. I just don't know if I can make it through that song.

MAMA WHEELIS. Honey, we gotta do it fer Buford. It was his last request.

LURLENE. I know. *(MAMA WHEELIS hugs her.)*

MAMA WHEELIS. Buford looked real good, so natural. Lester done a good job. Better than he done on Finwick. Lord, she looked awful.

(ORVILLE Enters from hallway entrance, his tie hasn't been tied properly.)

ORVILLE. I ain't goin' to the funeral. If all he left me was one measly buck, then I ain't goin' to his funeral.

LURLENE. Orville, please.

ORVILLE. No, I ain't goin'.

LURLENE. Orville, you've got to go. It wouldn't look right.

ORVILLE. I don't gotta do nothin'.

SARA LEE. Orville, I told yew that I was gonna split my share with yew and Lurlene.

ORVILLE. Then I'll go to yure funeral. I ain't goin' to his.

MAMA WHEELIS. Orville, yew gotta go to yure own daddy's funeral.

ORVILLE. *(As LURLENE straightens his tie; a little emotional.)* Marlene used to tie my tie. I cain't even tie my own damn tie. Lurlene, I never meant to hurt her.

LURLENE. I know. *(Hugging him.)* It's alright, Orville. I tied it. It looks real good. *(Kisses him.)* We love you, Orville.

MAMA WHEELIS. We need ta practice that song.

(EVALITA Enters from hallway in skin tight bright spandex pants and a flashy, fringy, low-cut blouse.)

EVALITA. I'm ready.

MAMA WHEELIS. Oh, my Lord.

LURLENE. Oh, dear.

SARA LEE. Evalita, it's about twenty minutes 'til we need ta be at Daddy's funeral.

EVALITA. I'm ready.

LURLENE. Yew can't wear that.

EVALITA. The hell I cain't. I can wear enythang I damn well please.

MAMA WHEELIS. Well it shows about as much respect as that trashy mouth of yures.

EVALITA. Do I look like I give a shit? Besides, that's a matter of opinion, Mama Wheelis. And I certainly don't live my life by the standards of Lowake, Texas.

LURLENE. You don't live your life by any standards.

EVALITA. Listen, Lurlene. I've had jest about enough.

SARA LEE. 'Bout time.

EVALITA. If I'm performin', I'm wearin' my stage clothes.

LURLENE. Evalita, this is the Baptist Church...not the Grand Ol' Opery.

MAMA WHEELIS. *(Suddenly remembering.)* Minnie Pearl. She was the one on the Hollywood Squares that sed that breakfast is the most important meal of the day.

ORVILLE. *(Looking at EVALITA.)* Well, I ain't goin'. I jest now decided fer sure.

MAMA WHEELIS. *(Goes and hugs ORVILLE.)* We need yure voice, honey. Buford wanted us all ta sang like we used to...all of us together. I wish Linnie Sue was here. She had the sweetest voice. Jest like a angel.

LURLENE. We're going to sing his favorite, "In the Garden." Just like when we were all kids. It was his last request.

SARA LEE. Except for that redhead.

MAMA WHEELIS. Bless 'is heart.

EVALITA. I'll sang somethin' solo. I ain't sangin' with ya'll.

LURLENE. We're all singing together. The service is planned, Evalita.

EVALITA. Well, yew can count me out. I don't sang with amateurs.

SARA LEE. Yew ought ta be ashamed of yureself. Goin' to your own daddy's funeral dressed like that.

EVALITA. Well, I'm not.

MAMA WHEELIS. Trash. Pure dee white trash.

LURLENE. Quite frankly, I'd be embarrassed to be seen with you.

EVALITA. *(Suddenly bursting into tears.)* Goddamnit! It's all I have to wear. I don't have enythang else. *(She rushes back down the hall.)*

SARA LEE. *(Running after her.)* Evalita.

EVALITA. Leave me alone. Jest leave me alone. *(She slams an O.S. door in SARA LEE'S face.)*

LURLENE. Oh, my goodness. I feel just awful.

MAMA WHEELIS. I'd been glad to loan her a shawl or an apron or somethin'.

(SARA LEE Enters from hallway.)

SARA LEE. She went in Daddy's room and locked the door. How come ever' time she's wrong we always end up feelin' sorry for her?

MAMA WHEELIS. I don't know, but we need ta practice that song.

SARA LEE. *(irritated)* Okay, Mama Wheelis. Let's practice the song.

LURLENE. Orville, are you going to help us?

ORVILLE. Hell, no.

MAMA WHEELIS. Well I giss that me, Sara Lee and Lurlene will jest have ta sang a trio.

LURLENE. *(Sits down at the piano; SARA LEE makes her way over and stands by MAMA WHEELIS behind LURLENE.)* Okay, let's give it a try.

SARA LEE. I'll sang alto.

LURLENE. I'll sing soprano.

MAMA WHEELIS. I'll sang whatever comes outta my mouth.

LURLENE, SARA LEE and MAMA WHEELIS. *(singing)* "I come to the garden alone, While the dew is still on the roses, And the voice I hear, Falling on my ear, The Son of God discloses." *(They continue as ORVILLE sits with his head down. He finally looks up, tears are streaming down his face.)*

ORVILLE. *(Singing softly along with his sisters.)* "And He walks with me, and He talks with me, And He tells me I am his own..." *(He goes over and stands by SARA LEE.)*

LURLENE, SARA LEE, MAMA WHEELIS and ORVILLE. "And the joy we share as we tarry there...None other has ever known. He speaks and the sound of his voice, Is so sweet the birds hush their singing..."

(As they continue to sing, EVALITA Enters from the hallway, wearing Daddy's old sweater over her low-cut blouse. She watches the others, then walks over to them, standing by ORVILLE.)

EVALITA. *(Starts singing along with the others, tears fill her eyes.)* ..."And the melody that he gave to me..."

LURLENE, SARA LEE, MAMA WHEELIS, ORVILLE and EVALITA. "...Within my heart is ringing. *(They all put their arms around each other.)* "And he walks with me, and He talks with me, And He tells me I am His own: And the joy we share as we tarry there, None other has ever known."

(As they sing the last few bars, the LIGHTS grow dimmer and dimmer and we hear CHILDREN'S VOICES singing the same song in the distance, gradually taking the place of their voices;

LURLENE turns around, joining hands with MAMA WHEELIS and EVALITA, forming an unbroken circle as the CHILDREN sing until:)

BLACKOUT

THE END

COSTUME PLOT

ACT I
SCENE 1

SARA LEE
Lee jeans
Western shirt
Sandals
Leather belt
Long earrings
Engagement ring
Timex wristwatch

LURLENE
Royal blue skirt
Royal blue blouse
White earrings
White belt
White beads
White shoes
White purse
Wedding band & diamond engagement ring
Watch

MAMA WHEELIS
Print house dress
Flowered handbag
Hairnet
Orthopedic white shoes
Torn knee-highs
Old watch
Wedding band

EVALITA
Denim short shorts
Halter
High heels
Cheap earrings and bracelets

HARMONY
Sleeveless jeans jacket (no shirt)
Old torn faded jeans
Long earrings and ear cuff
Leather arm bands
Red fringe belt
Indian choker necklace
Thongs

SCENE 2

SARA LEE
Same as Scene 1

LURLENE
Same as Scene 1

MAMA WHEELIS
Same as Scene 1

HARMONY
Same as Scene 1
Remove jacket; add red tank

EVALITA
Same as Scene 1

ORVILLE
Faded jeans
Striped short sleeve shirt
Cowboy boots
Dallas Cowboy baseball cap
Watch
Wedding band

BUFORD
Western dress hat
Western shirt
Western dress pants
Cowboy dress boots
Hospital bracelet
Wedding band

MARLENE
Mint green skirt
Full slip
Plaid blouse
Worn wedgies
Fake pearl earrings
Wedding band

SCENE 3

BUFORD
Same
No hat

HARMONY
Same

MAMA WHEELIS
Same
Add bib apron

MARLENE
Print flowered moo moo
Full slip (showing six inches)
Same wedgies
Two pink foam rollers
Same jewelry

SARA LEE
Western shirt, dressy
Western pants, polyester, tan, dressy
Long earrings
Leather purse
Leather belt
Cowboy boots
Same watch

LURLENE
Baby blue skirt
Baby blue blouse
Pink earrings
Pink belt
Pink purse
Pink shoes
Same watch

ACT II
SCENE 1

BUFORD
Same

2nd entrance
Robe and slippers

SARA LEE
Same
Add sunglasses

LURLENE
Same
Add sunglasses

ORVILLE
Same

EVALITA
Same
Harmony's jean jacket

MAMA WHEELIS
Calico house dress
Green flowered bib apron with pockets
Roll-down knee-highs
Straw hat
Sears tennis shoes
Same jewelry

SCENE 2

MARLENE
Lavender skirt
Pink & white striped blouse
White sandals
Same jewelry

HARMONY
Same

ORVILLE
Same

MAMA WHEELIS
Flowered print house coat
Slippers
Same jewelry
(Most of funeral scene's costume underneath)

SARA LEE
Pink bath robe
Blue shower cap
House shoes
Full lacy slip *(to prepare for last scene)*

LURLENE
Same

EVALITA
Same

Loose Harmony jacket

SCENE 3

MAMA WHEELIS
Black polyester dated dress
Black Sunday hat
Black orthopedic shoes
Full slip

LURLENE
Nice black silk blouse
Stylish black skirt
Hose
Slip
Black pumps
Black beads
Pearl earrings
Black purse

SARA LEE
Black dress, not too stylish
Black pumps
Full slip
Watch

ORVILLE
Western brown dress pants
Tan dress shirt
Striped wide tie

Same boots
Belt with cowboy buckle

EVALITA
Purple spandex pants
Purple leotard, trimmed in sequin fringe
Silver long earrings
Silver bracelets
Silver shoes

Second Entrance
Add Daddy's sweater

PROPERTY PLOT

ONSTAGE
Couch
  afghan
  checker board underneath
Stuffed chair
Rocking chair
Footstool
Coffee table
  Bible
  wicker container containing checkers
  Sara Lee's cigarettes
  Sara Lee's lighter
  ashtray
  candy dish full of candy orange slices
  small photo albums
Small side table
  box of Kleenex
  family picture
Air-conditioner in window
Upright piano
  hymnals
  pictures of family
  radio
  telephone
  telephone/address book
Piano bench
  hymnals

        sheet music
        misc. junk
Bill holder over telephone
Old family pictures on wall
Bullhorns on wall
Inside closet
        hook for hat
        coats
        shirts
        box of junk
        blanket
Dining table
Dining chairs
        2 on stage
        1 in hallway
        2 in kitchen
Knickknack shelf
        small demitasse cup collection
        misc. knickknacks
Cabinet for dishes
        7 plates
        7 place settings of silver
        5 cups and saucers
        tablecloth
        napkin holder on top
        Jesus fan
        wicker chicken with bobbypins
        bottle opener
        mirror over cabinet
Pictures on wall
        2 old oval family pictures (in living room)

old oval family picture (in hallway)

small picture on other side of knickknack shelf

4 high school pictures of Turnovers on back kitchen wall,
one of Jimbo, one of Lurlene's boys as small
children

Jesus (non-Catholic, over dining table)

Linnie Sue's picture, surrounded in frame by sym-
pathy cards (over dining table, by knickknack
shelf)

Lord's prayer (over dining table)

OFFSTAGE

BY FRONT DOOR

Medicine bottle with pills (Orville)

Case of beer (Orville)

Six-pack of beer (Evalita)

Demo tape (Harmony)

Rice cakes (Harmony)

Covered bowl (to be handed to Mama Wheelis)

Designer suitcase (Lurlene)

Lurlene's white purse

Pictures of boys

2 ugly suitcases (Marlene)

IN KITCHEN

Cigarettes (Sara Lee)

Matches (Sara Lee)

2 cup towels

Aprons

2 hot pads

2 cups of coffee (brought on by Sara Lee for herself &
Lurlene)

Ice tea (brought on by Mama Wheelis for Evalita)
4 Lone Star bottles full of water (brought from kit-
        chen by Marlene)

SUPPER SCENE:
8 plastic glasses (to be brought out by Harmony &
        Marlene, setting table)
*Cornbread (for supper scene)
*Roast, carrots, whole potatoes
*Black-eyed peas
*Mashed potatoes
Gravy boat
Ladle
*can be fake

Milk of Magnesia bottle
Spoon (for Mom)

BREAKFAST SCENE:
Creamer
Cream
Sugar bowl
Sugar
Salt & pepper shakers
Coffee pot
Coffee
2 empty bowls (grits, misc.)
Platter (of fake eggs)
Opaque glass (for Marlene's Herbalean)
Teaspoon (for Marlene's Herbalean)
Bacon

Bisquits
Gravy boat (same as for supper scene)
Ladle (same as for supper scene)

Tray (Lurlene takes to Buford)
Plate with cover (Lurlene takes to Buford)

Bowl (for Mama Wheelis to snap beans or peel
     potatoes)
Beans or potatoes (Mama Wheelis)

MARLENE & HARMONY'S SNACK:
Bread
Roastbeef
Pie
Pie pan
Miracle Whip
Knife
Fork
Napkins
Ice tea

Strongbox (Orville)
  Inside:
      bronzed baby shoes
      arrowhead
      will
      report card
      newspaper obituary clipping
      documents and papers

Key for strongbox lock (Harmony)
Hairpins (Evalita, Marlene, Mama Wheelis, Lurlene,
　Sara Lee)
Hairspray (Sara Lee)
Rattail comb (Sara Lee)

In the Garden

C. A. M.

C. Austin Miles

1. I come to the garden a - lone, While the dew is still on the
2. He speaks, and the sound of His voice Is so sweet the birds hush their
3. I'd stay in the garden with him Though the night around me be

ros - es, And the voice I hear, Fall-ing on my ear, The
sing - ing, And the mel - o - dy That He gave to me, With-
fall - ing, But He bids me go; Thro' the voice of woe His

Chorus

Son of God dis - clos - es.
in my heart is ring - ing. And He walks with me, and He
voice to me is call - ing.

talks with me, And He tells me I am His own; And the

joy we share as we tar - ry there, None oth-er has ev - er known.

The Unclouded Day

J. K. A.

Rev. J. K. Alwood

1. O they tell me of a home far be-yond the skies, O they
2. O they tell me of a home where my friends have gone, O they
3. O they tell me of a King in His beau-ty there, And they
4. O they tell me that He smiles on His chil-dren there, And His

tell me of a home far a-way; O they tell me of a home
tell me of that land far a-way, Where the tree of life
tell me that mine eyes shall be-hold Where He sits on the throne
smile drives their sor-rows all a-way; And they tell me that no tears

D. S.—*O they tell me of a home*

where no storm-clouds rise, O they tell me of an un-cloud-ed day.
in e-ter-nal bloom Sheds its fra-grance thro' the un-cloud-ed day.
that is whit-er than snow, In the cit-y that is made of gold.
ev-er come a-gain, In that love-ly land of un-cloud-ed day.

where no storm-clouds rise, O they tell me of an un-cloud-ed day.

CHORUS

D. S.

O the land of cloud-less day, O the land of an un-cloud-ed day;

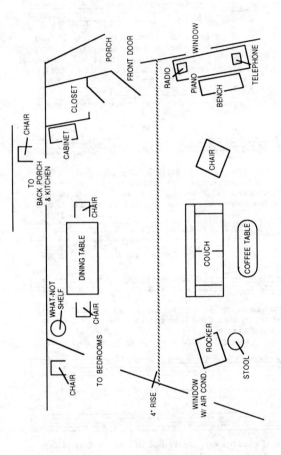

SCENE DESIGN
"DADDY'S DYIN' WHO'S GOT THE WILL?"

NEWELL ALEXANDER, DESIGNER

ORIGINAL PRODUCTION, THEATRE/THEATER, HOLLYWOOD, CA

A Breeze from The Gulf

MART CROWLEY

(Little Theatre) Drama

The author of "The Boys in the Band" takes us on a journey back to a small Mississippi town to watch a 15-year-old boy suffer through adolescence to adulthood and success as a writer. His mother is a frilly southern doll who has nothing to fall back on when her beauty fades. She develops headaches and other physical problems, while the asthmatic son turns to dolls and toys at an age when other boys are turning to sports. The traveling father becomes withdrawn, takes to drink; and mother takes to drugs to kill the pain of the remembrances of things past. She eventually ends in an asylum, and the father in his fumbling way tries to tell the son to live the life he must.

"The boy is plunged into a world of suffering he didn't create. . . . One of the most electrifying plays I've seen in the past few years . . . Scenes boil and hiss . . . The dialogue goes straight to the heart." Reed, Sunday News.

ECHOES

N. RICHARD NASH

(All Groups) Drama
2 Men, 1 Woman, Interior

A young man and woman build a low-keyed paradise of happiness within an asylum, only to have it shattered by the intrusion of the outside world. The two characters search, at times agonizingly to determine the difference between illusion and reality. The effort is lightened at times by moments of shared love and "pretend" games, like decorating Christmas trees that are not really there. The theme of love, vulnerable to the surveillances of the asylum, and the ministrations of the psychiatrist, (a non-speaking part) seems as fragile in the constrained setting as it often is in the outside world.

". . . even with the tragic, sombre theme there is a note of hope and possible release and the situations presented specifically also have universal applications to give it strong effect . . . intellectual, but charged with emotion."—Reed.

Other Publications for Your Interest

TALKING WITH...
(LITTLE THEATRE)
By JANE MARTIN

11 women—Bare stage

Here, at last, is the collection of eleven extraordinary monologues for eleven actresses which had them on their feet cheering at the famed Actors Theatre of Louisville—audiences, critics and, yes, even jaded theatre professionals. The mysteriously pseudonymous Jane Martin is truly a "find", a new writer with a wonderfully idiosyncratic style, whose characters alternately amuse, move and frighten us always, however, speaking to use from the depths of their souls. The characters include a baton twirler who has found God through twirling; a fundamentalist snake handler, an ex-rodeo rider crowded out of the life she has cherished by men in 3-piece suits who want her to dress up "like Minnie damn Mouse in a tutu"; an actress willing to go to any length to get a job; and an old woman who claims she once saw a man with "cerebral walrus" walk into a McDonald's and be healed by a Big Mac. "Eleven female monologues, of which half a dozen verge on brilliance."—London Guardian. "Whoever (Jane Martin) is, she's a writer with an original imagination."—Village Voice. "With Jane Martin, the monologue has taken on a new poetic form, intensive in its method and revelatory in its impact."—Philadelphia Inquirer. "A dramatist with an original voice . . . (these are) tales about enthusiasms that become obsessions, eccentric confessionals that levitate with religious symbolism and gladsome humor."—N.Y. Times. *Talking With* . . . is the 1982 winner of the American Theatre Critics Association Award for Best Regional Play.   (#22009)

HAROLD AND MAUDE
(ADVANCED GROUPS—COMEDY)
By COLIN HIGGINS

9 men, 8 women—Various settings

Yes: *the Harold and Maude!* This is a stage adaptation of the wonderful movie about the suicidal 19 year-old boy who finally learns how to truly *live* when he meets up with that delightfully whacky octogenarian, Maude. Harold is the proverbial Poor Little Rich Kid. His alienation has caused him to attempt suicide several times, though these attempts are more cries for attention than actual attempts. His peculiar attachment to Maude, whom he meets at a funeral (a mutual passion), is what saves him—and what captivates us. This new stage version, a hit in France directed by the internationally-renowned Jean-Louis Barrault, will certainly delight both afficionados of the film and new-comers to the story. "Offbeat upbeat comedy."—Christian Science Monitor.   (#10032)

Other Publications for Your Interest

MAGIC TIME
(LITTLE THEATRE—COMEDY)

By JAMES SHERMAN

5 men, 3 women—Interior

Off Broadway audiences and the critics enjoyed and praised this engaging backstage comedy about a troupe of professional actors (non-Equity) preparing to give their last performance of the summer in *Hamlet*. Very cleverly the backstage relationships mirror the onstage ones. For instance, Larry Mandell (Laertes) very much resents the performance of David Singer (Hamlet), as he feels *he* should have had the role. Also, he is secretly in love with Laurie Black (Ophelia)—who is living with David. David, meanwhile, is holding a mirror up to nature, but not to himself—and Laurie is trying to get him to be honest with her about his feelings. There's also a Horatio who has a thriving career in TV commercials; a Polonius who gave up acting to have a family and teach high school, but who has decidedly second thoughts, and a Gertrude and Claudius who are married in *real* life. This engaging play is an absolute *must* for all non-Equity groups, such as colleges, community theatres, and non-Equity pros or semi-pros. "There is an artful innocence in 'Magic Time' . . . It is also delightful."—N.Y. Times. ". . . captivating little backstage comedy . . . it is entirely winning . . . boasts one of the most entertaining band of Shakespearean players I've run across."—N.Y. Daily News. (#15028)

BADGERS
(LITTLE THEATRE—COMEDY)

By DONALD WOLLNER

6 men, 2 women—Interior, w/insert

"'Badgers! . . . opened the season at the Manhattan Punchline while Simon and Garfunkel were offering a concert in Central Park. In tandem, the two events were a kind of déjà vu for the 60's, when all things seemed possible, even revolution. As we watch 'Badgers' we can hear a subliminal 'Sounds of Silence'."—N.Y. Times. The time is 1967. The place is the University of Wisconsin during the Dow Chemical sit-in/riots. This cross-section of college campus life in that turbulent decade focuses on the effect of the events on the characters: "Wollner's amiable remembrance adds up to a sort of campus roll-call—here are radicalized kids from Eastern high schools, 'WASP' accountancy majors who didn't make Harvard or Penn. Most significant is the playwright's contention that none were touched lightly by those times . . . he has a strong sense of the canvas he's drawing on."—Soho Weekly News. If you loved *Moonchildren,* you're certain to love this "wry and gentle look at a toubled time" (Bergen Record). (#3998)

Other Publications for Your Interest

HUSBANDRY
(LITTLE THEATRE—DRAMA)

By PATRICK TOVATT

2 men, 2 women—Interior

At its recent world premiere at the famed Actors Theatre of Louisville, this enticing new drama moved an audience of theatre professionals up off their seats and on to their feet to cheer. Mr. Tovatt has given us an insightful drama about what is happening to the small, family farm in America—and what this means for the future of the country. The scene is a farmhouse whose owners are on the verge of losing their farm. They are visited by their son and his wife, who live "only" eight hours' drive away. The son has a good job in the city, and his wife does, too. The son, Harry, is really put on the horns of a dilemma when he realizes that he is his folks' only hope. The old man can't go it alone anymore—and he needs his son. Pulling at him from the other side is his wife, who does not want to leave her job and uproot her family to become a farm wife. *Husbandry*, then, is ultimately about what it means to be a *husband*—both in the farm and in the family sense. *Variety* praised the "delicacy of Tovatt's dialogue", and called the play "a literate exploration of family responsibilities in a mobile society." Said *Time*: "The play simmers so gently for so long, as each potential confrontation is deflected with Chekhovian shrugs and silences, that when it boils into hostility it sears the audience."   (#10169)

CLARA'S PLAY
(LITTLE THEATRE—DRAMA)

By JOHN OLIVE

3 men, 1 woman—Exterior

Clara, an aging spinster, lives alone in a remote farmhouse. She is the last surviving member of one of the area's most prominent families. It is summer, 1915. Enter an immigrant, feisty soul named Sverre looking for a few days' work before moving on. But Clara's farm needs more than just a few days' work, and Sverre stays on to help Clara fix up and run the farm. It soon becomes clear unscrupulous local businessmen are bilking Clara out of money and hope to gain control of her property. Sverre agrees to stay on to help Clara keep her family's property. "A story of determination, loyalty. It has more than a measure of love, of resignation, of humor and loyalty."—Chicago Sun-Times. "A playwright of unusual sensitivity in delineating character and exploring human relationships." —Chicago Tribune. "Gracefully-written, with a real sense of place."—Village Voice. A recent success both at Chicago's fine Wisdom Bridge Theatre and at the Great American Play Festival of the world-reknowned Actors Theatre of Louisville; and, on tour, starring Jean Stapleton.   (#5076)

Other Publications for Your Interest

A WEEKEND NEAR MADISON
(LITTLE THEATRE—COMIC DRAMA)
By KATHLEEN TOLAN

2 men, 3 women—Interior

This recent hit from the famed Actors Theatre of Louisville, a terrific ensemble play about male-female relationships in the 80's, was praised by *Newsweek* as "warm, vital, glowing . . . full of wise ironies and unsentimental hopes". The story concerns a weekend reunion of old college friends now in their early thirties. The occasion is the visit of Vanessa, the queen bee of the group, who is now the leader of a lesbian/feminist rock band. Vanessa arrives at the home of an old friend who is now a psychiatrist hand in hand with her naif-like lover, who also plays in the band. Also on hand are the psychiatrist's wife, a novelist suffering from writer's block; and his brother, who was once Vanessa's lover and who still loves her. In the course of the weekend, Vanessa reveals that she and her lover desperately want to have a child—and she tries to persuade her former male lover to father it, not understanding that he might have some feelings about the whole thing. *Time Magazine* heard "the unmistakable cry of an infant hit . . . Playwright Tolan's work radiates promise and achievement." (#25051)

PASTORALE
(LITTLE THEATRE—COMEDY)
By DEBORAH EISENBERG

3 men, 4 women—Interior
(plus 1 or 2 bit parts and 3 optional extras)

"Deborah Eisenberg is one of the freshest and funniest voices in some seasons."—Newsweek. Somewhere out in the country Melanie has rented a house and in the living room she, her friend Rachel who came for a weekend but forgets to leave, and their school friend Steve (all in their mid-20s) spend nearly a year meandering through a mental landscape including such concerns as phobias, friendship, work, sex, slovenliness and epistemology. Other people happen by: Steve's young girlfriend Celia, the virtuous and annoying Edie, a man who Melanie has picked up in a bar, and a couple who appear during an intense conversation and observe the sofa is on fire. The lives of the three friends inevitably proceed and eventually draw them, the better prepared perhaps by their months on the sofa, in separate directions. "The most original, funniest new comic voice to be heard in New York theater since Beth Henley's 'Crimes of the Heart.'"—N.Y. Times. "A very funny, stylish comedy."—The New Yorker. "Wacky charm and wayward wit."—New York Magazine. "Delightful."—N.Y. Post. "Uproarious . . . the play is a world unto itself, and it spins."—N.Y. Sunday Times. (#18016)

Other Publications for Your Interest

THE CURATE SHAKESPEARE
AS YOU LIKE IT
(LITTLE THEATRE—COMEDY)

By DON NIGRO

4 men, 3 women—Bare stage

This extremely unusual and original piece is subtitled: "The record of one company's attempt to perform the play by William Shakespeare". When the very prolific Mr. Nigro was asked by a professional theatre company to adapt *As You Like It* so that it could be performed by a company of seven he, of course, came up with a completely original play about a rag-tag group of players comprised of only seven actors led by a dotty old curate who nonetheless must present Shakespeare's play; and the dramatic interest, as well as the comedy, is in their hilarious attempts to impersonate all of Shakespeare's multitude of characters. The play has had numerous productions nationwide, all of which have come about through word of mouth. We are very pleased to make this "underground comic classic" widely available to theatre groups who like their comedy wide open and theatrical. (#5742)

SEASCAPE WITH SHARKS
AND DANCER
(LITTLE THEATRE—DRAMA)

By DON NIGRO

1 man, 1 woman—Interior

This is a fine new play by an author of great talent and promise. We are very glad to be introducing Mr. Nigro's work to a wide audience with *Seascape With Sharks and Dancer*, which comes directly from a sold-out, critically acclaimed production at the world-famous Oregon Shakespeare Festival. The play is set in a beach bungalow. The young man who lives there has pulled a lost young woman from the ocean. Soon, she finds herself trapped in his life and torn between her need to come to rest somewhere and her certainty that all human relationships turn eventually into nightmares. The struggle between his tolerant and gently ironic approach to life and her strategy of suspicion and attack becomes a kind of war about love and creation which neither can afford to lose. In other words, this is quite an offbeat, wonderful love story. We would like to point out that the play also contains a wealth of excellent *monologue* and *scene material*. (#21060)